WHEN
ALL
ELSE
FAILS

Finding Solutions
to Your
Most Persistent
Management Problems

by
Kevin E. O'Connor
and
Frank C. Bucaro

Ritmar Publishing
722 Canyon Lane
Elgin, IL 60123-2522
(1-800-462-6657)

ISBN 0-9631170-4-1

LCCN 91-67912

A practical little book filled with one big idea
. . . and dozens of little ones . . . to help you
work, manage, live, and love more effectively.

"You will never know what you can do until you do it."
—Rudolf Dreikurs

Dedication

For Rita O'Connor and Mary Ann Bucaro.
For all of your support, encouragement, and faith in our
abilities, potential, and vision . . . You've helped us become
more focused—when all else fails!

Acknowledgements

We'd like to thank:

- Our families for their support and encouragement.

- Our graduate students and our customers who allow us to help them access the solutions that are already within them.

- Don Houde, Irene Friend, Pat Render, and Marianne Weakley whose early vote of confidence helped us launch a career.

- Rick Batt for his enthusiasm, encouragement, and his openness to new ideas.

- Kris Loewe whose transcription and initial editing solved many problems before we even knew they existed.

- John Walter and Jane Peller, our mentors and teachers in solution focused thinking.

- Steve deShazer who pioneered solution focused theory so life would be easier for individuals, marriages, and families . . . and now customers and businesses.

- Michele Weiner-Davis whose focus on marriage and partnership has accelerated theory into popular practice.

- Michael Popkin whose popular version of psychology has helped hundreds of thousands of parents and their children.

- Richard Royal Kopp for his research, metaphorical thinking, and his unique approach to psychology in business.

And, of course, Alfred Adler and Rudolf Dreikurs, collaborators and pioneers in the psychology of the human person.

Table of Contents

Dedication

Acknowledgements

Chapter One
A New Approach to Management 1

Chapter Two
The Solution Is Inside 5

Chapter Three
The Problem with Problems 9

Chapter Four
Encouraging Solutions: What's It Like
When It's Not Like That? 13

Chapter Five
Human Behavior: Principles for Solutions 17

Chapter Six
A Short Course in Solution Development 23

Chapter Seven
It's Not Always Easy to Identify 33

Chapter Eight
Miracles Do Happen . . .
When We Make Them Happen 37

Chapter Nine
Solution Focused Conflict 41

Chapter Ten
Even "Junk" Works 45

Chapter Eleven
Collaboration 47

Chapter Twelve
To Begin 51

Chapter Thirteen
From Conflict to Cooperation 57

Chapter Fourteen
The Role of Feelings 65

Chapter Fifteen
Cooperation Is Inevitable
(If We See It That Way) 69

Chapter Sixteen
Before All Else Fails—DSD 71

Chapter Seventeen
Sometimes Don't Do Anything 73

Chapter Eighteen
An Additional Strategy—DTO 75

Chapter Nineteen
Person to Person Corollaries 77

Chapter Twenty
Three Helpful Reminders 83

Chapter Twenty-One
Tactics That Work 91

Chapter Twenty-Two
Cooperation and the Feeling of Equality 97

Chapter Twenty-Three
Your Answer Is Inside the Question 101

Chapter Twenty-Four
Insuring Success: Some (Almost) Fail-Safe
Approaches to Working with Another 107

Chapter Twenty-Five
The Part He Doesn't Let Out Too Much 109

Chapter Twenty-Six
We Should Talk More about This 111

Chapter Twenty-Seven
Make the Second Call 113

Chapter Twenty-Eight
When in Doubt, Ask "What Did I Forget?" 115

Chapter Twenty-Nine
Take a Mental Sabbatical 117

Chapter Thirty
Declare Bankruptcy . . .
Emotionally That Is! 119

Chapter Thirty-One
How Was I Different Today . . .
And What Difference Did That Seem to Make? . 121

Chapter Thirty-Two
"When I Treat Him in a More
Businesslike Fashion, We Get More Done" 123

Chapter Thirty-Three
Watch for "The Trance" 125

Chapter Thirty-Four
Don't Throw That Old Picture Out . . .
Reframe It! 129

Chapter Thirty-Five
Flag the Minefield 131

Chapter Thirty-Six
Storm the Back Door 133

Chapter Thirty-Seven
Can You Tell the Difference? 135

Chapter Thirty-Eight
To Avoid Failure, Predict the Relapse 139

Chapter Thirty-Nine
Notice What You Notice 143

Bibliography and Resources 145

About the Authors 149

CHAPTER ONE

A New Approach to Management

*"If you continue to do what you are doing
—you'll always get what you got."*
—Dr. Lee Robinson
Utah School For The Blind

Gaining Access

If executives and managers could have anything they wanted, what might that be? No doubt they would substantially increase their influence within the hierarchy of their companies. All managers would like to have important employees listen to them, respect deadlines, and fulfill requests without unnecessary delays and snags. Perhaps most people want those in other departments to take their advice more often. Surely, all executives and managers wish for more productive meetings. And they would certainly like to change the behavior of the difficult people in their lives, at work and at home.

Does this sound impossible—too good to be true? Without exaggeration, all these changes are possible by using what we call Solution Focused Management.

Solution Focused Management is a simple way to gain access to already existing solutions by focusing on the *exceptions* to any given problem. For example:

In his work with a newly-appointed president, a vice-president was consistently encountering conflict. His more relaxed, interpersonal style of management was in sharp contrast to the president's very direct, aggressive, and task oriented style. As things became worse, communication suffered—as did mutual trust. A very real tug-of-war accelerated.

The vice-president attempted to be more conciliatory, but his changes had little impact. First, he listened more. That seemed to make things worse. Then he became more proactive—even arguing more—only to be "outwitted" (as he put it) by her direct and dominant style.

Discouraged and near defeat, he spoke with a consultant who used a model focusing on solutions. When the consultant asked, "What's it like when the two of you are not this way?", the vice-president realized a solution was already inside of him. "Last Tuesday we had a very fine meeting. The only thing different was I had my legal pad with me. I was taking notes on the meeting so I could write an article for the corporate newsletter. I don't know if that made a difference or not—but it's the only thing *I* did differently. It's funny, *she* was different, very different: still direct, still businesslike and aggressive, but no venom. We got the work done without any fight."

Needless to say, his yellow pad became his constant companion.

There was one exception to this vice-president's experience. Without looking at it or searching for it, he probably would have skipped over this one exception, seeing it as an accident or fluke. But by recognizing it as a *working exception*, he was able to use it in his dealings with the president.

Gaining Competence

There is an infinite supply of solutions to problems. We need to consult our own experience in a special way to find them. This book will show you what this special way is and how you can apply it. Expertise can be learned; solutions can be found.

CHAPTER TWO

The Solution Is Inside

Gaining access to the solution already within him was the challenge for the vice-president in conflict with the newly appointed president. The solution was an "inside job" for one—a changed relationship for both.

Getting Started . . . Now

In addition to answers already existing within us, there are solution strategies which work for a wide variety of situations. The following is an example of this approach, and it applies to numerous situations needing specific solutions.

Meetings are a chronic issue for many busy executives and managers. Despite their best efforts, many run into "meeting malaise." They're too long, too chatty, or misdirected. They start late, run over the allotted time, and can be too detailed or too general to do any good.

We recommend a number of strategies to change the negative characteristics of meetings. There are ways to find solutions without blaming others or launching into a lengthy analysis of the problem. You might begin by using any of the following techniques for your own meetings—then notice what's different. (Why wait to read this whole book? Start your changes now!)

- Over the next week or two, quietly take notes of the things that happen at meetings that you would like to continue to see. It's that simple. Take notes and see what happens.

- Do something different. It could be anything. Even a small, seemingly insignificant thing can make a meeting distinct. Observe what happens that's different or better. You might, for example, announce a new starting time—9:04 A.M. instead of 9:00 A.M. Sit in a new place around the table, invite one new person to the meeting, change the location, bring in food (or cancel the customary order for it), even remove the chairs. After having done this one thing unusually, observe what happens that's better or just different.

- Ask yourself what Steve deShazer calls the "miracle question." That is, if a miracle were to happen tonight and the meeting were improved, what would be different or better? More importantly, ask, "What would I be doing as a result of this difference?" At your next meeting, act *as if* that miracle had happened. Again notice what is different or better.

All three of these suggestions can help you gain access to the *exceptions* to the problem: in effect, the *solutions*. The best part is these suggestions bypass the dreary business of problem identification, discussion, strategy making, and follow-up. They focus on getting things solved!

Becoming Solution Focused

So, whether we concentrate on the exceptions (solutions!) already within us, or use a specific and generic solution strategy, the important feature is that we become *solution-focused*. The beauty of Solution Focused Management is:

Its simplicity—anyone can do it.

Its directness—solution seeking bypasses a problem focus.

Its subtlety—the obvious cooperation of others isn't needed, only their natural cooperation.

Its reliability—it works! It works everywhere.

You could easily apply any of the above techniques to a small business, General Motors, or the local Rotary club. They will work equally well at your dinner table, a parent-teacher conference, or a church committee. Use them on the pushy time-share salesperson or even to resolve a complaint at your local grocery store.

The basic premise of *When All Else Fails* is a new approach to solving both chronic and acute problems. This approach focuses on solutions already within us or around us—solutions we fail to take note of and use. A sample of some specific applications would be employer-employee relationships, morale building, conflict resolution, goal coaching, plus individual and group problem solving. Other possibilities include: budgetary and financial concerns, personnel developments, performance appraisals, time management, and project management. This is an idea that focuses on people-building and people-management . . . *not* on people-manipulation.

We wish you well as *you* become a solution focused manager.

> *"We cannot build on weakness—only on strength. To eliminate criticism and minimize mistakes can be both a great challenge to the manager and a great relief to those managed."*
>
> —Adapted from Rudolf Dreikurs
> and Vicki Soltz

CHAPTER THREE

The Problem
with Problems

*"The greatest calamity that could befall a
person is to have sight and fail to see."*
—Helen Keller

Consider

A manager whose secretary routinely makes sloppy
errors on what seem to be only the important docu-
ments.

An entry-level manager frustrated over an employee who argues at every turn, is openly stubborn, and
resists most attempts to elicit cooperation.

A professional ball player in a mid-season slump.

A 5 ½-year-old having temper tantrums in the
mornings before the kindergarten bus arrives.

A husband good-naturedly trying to have fun with
his wife—who is preoccupied, stressed out, and
overly concerned about her job's demands.

A mother, wanting to have some "family time" at dinner, watching her teenagers leave the house quickly after every meal.

A Management Information Systems team with contradictory opinions about the problem that affects them all.

Big and small, problems are the "stuff of life": at home, at work, with ourselves. Particularly in business, they come in many sizes, shapes, and levels of intensity. From routine paperwork to hostile takeovers, from conflicts between management and labor to job security (or insecurity!), from managing adults to structuring exciting programs in marketing—all pose formidable challenges to business leaders.

Our ability to solve these business related problems and the other demands of life has, in the past, hinged on diagnosing the problem, understanding its causes, developing alternative responses, and following through with a newly implemented plan. Sounds good. It even works well—sometimes. In short, the way we solved the problem depended upon how well we came to grips with it. That is, until recently.

A new method is being developed to replace the age-old "problem with problems." The new system helps us avoid getting stuck with old techniques.

Traditional Methods

Let's look at the traditional outline for problem resolution.

- *Defining the Problem.* Why is the hardest task the first? As one corporate vice-president said when he came in for a consultation, "If I knew precisely what was wrong, I wouldn't need to talk to you!" The traditional method for problem solving focuses first on the ins and outs of the difficulty. In addition to defining the problem, we fully investigate what's wrong, describe it in detail, and generally consume ourselves with the past.

In counseling, we listen on and on as the person speaks in the past tense. In meetings, we hear repetitive opinions about what went wrong. We interview associates with empathy and sympathy (sometimes we're glad it's not us!). Actually, defining the problem can easily get out of hand and discourage even our best efforts.

- *Asking for Help.* This step is difficult and, though sometimes necessary, it too can be confusing. Depending upon who you ask, you may find out, too late, what you should have done. This is a humbling experience. Asking for help may come before the problem definition stage or after.

  In any event, *who* you ask for help is far more important than *when* you ask. Inviting a collaboration can help or hurt, can develop or discourage, can inspire confidence or trigger confusion. In traditional problem solving, we too often look to the other as "the expert."

- *Developing Alternatives.* This can be a stupefying process. Trying to think of another way, and coming up blank, is often worse than being discouraged. Traditional problem solving has emphasized "brainstorming" a—no-holds-barred, no-evaluation listing of possible (and some seemingly impossible) solutions. Meant to generate an abundant flow of ideas, this step often requires a group effort with a good facilitator. A manager once commented, "Eighty percent of the ideas are too wild to work and the other twenty percent I've tried!" Not everyone has had the same negative experience with this technique, but it can be a potential source of frustration.

- *Following Through.* This step can often be the toughest. Simply put, it's hard to change, and sometimes even harder to have the staying power to keep the change going. This step is the most insidious of them all. We

11

have a long-range goal: To do things the "right way" or the "preferred way." Yet change is difficult, so we can wind up off course.

The last and most significant aspect of the problem-with-problem-solving is how discouraging it can be to actually solve problems. By the time all is resolved, you're exhausted, not elated. You're usually feeling tense rather than terrific. It's all quite laborious and confusing and, we believe, unnecessary.

A New Way

Imagine what you could do with your employees, your boss, your children, your neighbors, yourself, even your spouse, if you could bypass this discouraging process all together! What if you could concentrate on concrete solutions that really work, are easy to understand, and are natural to implement? *The good news is that these solutions are already within you, and you can gain access to them.*

CHAPTER FOUR

Encouraging Solutions: What's It Like When It's Not Like That?

Steve deShazer, a Milwaukee—based counselor and researcher, has developed a remarkable system to help *solutions* take priority over problems. Here's how it works. DeShazer asserts that solutions already exist within us. We just don't notice when these solutions work; therefore, we don't consciously recognize our need to apply more of them more often.

DeShazer believes that in every situation there are natural forces, and within every individual, natural strengths, that can lead directly to pre-existing solutions. The solutions already exist. (We see them as *exceptions* to the problem.) Therefore, we call the management process for solving problems with this new method, *Solution Focused Management.*

The Solution Focused Manager

The solution focused manager can effect great changes in cooperation by pointing out those times when the problem

13

doesn't occur. To this manager, the exceptional positive times are proof of the workability of a given situation, despite current setbacks or problems. To this manager, the exceptional times are those instances which need repetition. And these exceptional times are really "solution focused times". This manager knows the exceptional times are not accidental moments; they are just the easily forgotten ones. The solution focused manager is the one who looks past problems to what already exists, if only in a microscopic way.

A manager, Jim, led a group of twelve in weekly meetings lasting from one to three hours. As expected, some meetings were more productive than others. Productivity was, in Jim's opinion, on a downward cycle as time went on. Over a two month period, the productive meetings became the exception rather than the rule.

A detailed analysis of past meetings proved confusing. There seemed no rhyme or reason for either the productive or the unproductive meetings. Jim decided to keep an eye on those meetings (or even moments) when things did seem to be moving in a constructive way. As he observed the group, he noticed the productivity followed an action of his. He usually began the meeting by serving donuts and coffee, but bagels and juice opened one particularly positive and memorable meeting. Even with his late arrival one week, he noticed his assistant had a more "take charge" attitude than usual.

Jim would usually jump in, make a quick decision, and effectively veto further dissent. During one highly charged, emotional discussion, he stayed silent. This allowed the discussion to run its course. He was especially pleased that the decision made by the group was a good one.

As he observed meetings over the next two months, it became clear to Jim that whenever he was different, *in almost any way*, the meeting was different. He ceased his complaints about his staff and he focused on self-change. Most telling of all for him, he gave himself time to notice what was different. The *exceptions* pointed the way for this manager, and his exceptional behavior gave him more influence over his future.

Try being different too, *in almost any way*, and then notice what's different. It matters less what you do and more that you do something in order to succeed.

In your work life or at home, pick one situation that hasn't changed, and then *change you*. Note what else changes!

CHAPTER FIVE

Human Behavior: Principles for Solutions

Solution Focused Management, as illustrated by this typical example, is based on three simple but important principles of human behavior.

1. *All life is interpersonal.* We live and work with others. Few of our problems or our solutions are *not* interpersonal. Problems and solutions happen between people. When one person changes, so does the other.
2. Our *interpersonal interactions are maintained* by a unique set of inner talents which we use, for good or ill, to influence others. Over time a pattern—a unique style—develops. This style, though similar to that of others, is unique to us. We have the power to influence our problems and solutions by using our style.
3. By *harnessing our talents* and that unique pattern of interactions that works for us, we can expand our repertoire of responses to problems confronting us.

These principles of human behavior are not new. But what they tell us about ourselves is profound. We are choice-making, unique, and communal creatures who can influence one another through simple *self-change.*

Problems and Solutions

From these well-known principles, we would like to add the following.

1. *Problems happen.* A simple fact of life: Things don't always go the way we want them to. Sometimes they don't go at all! But many of us think problems need not have happened, shouldn't happen, or when they do, are insurmountable. Our approach is simple: problems happen. Our challenge is not to eliminate the problems, but to illuminate their possible solutions.

2. *Solutions exist.* A new concept addresses the solutions that already exist within us and our experience. Although we have problems in our daily life, we also have specific times when we don't have those difficulties. Problem employees cooperate—sometimes. Authoritarian leaders consult with us—sometimes. Argumentative spouses agree with our views—sometimes. The fact that the "sometimes" occurrences happen is testimony that solutions occur between people, even if they go unnoticed.

3. *Focus is the key.* One of the most frustrating activities of problem solving is a negative focus. Even with the best intentions, focusing on the problem can be debilitating and discouraging. But by strictly *focusing on solutions*, especially the ones we already have at our disposal, we can be revived and renewed.

A Way Past Problems

Solution focused theory has been developed, primarily by Steve deShazer, since 1978. Essentially, deShazer discovered the following:

1. Solutions happen when interactions between people are changed.
2. People have all the resources they need for change. The helper need only assist them in discovering the solution. It is already present within.
3. The meanings we give to events are not static. How we label and relabel is often a first step to solution. A "difficult" employee could also be seen as "a challenge" or "in need of closer supervision" or as one who is "frank and honest."
4. Only small changes and reasonable goals are necessary for big changes and fulfilled goals to happen.
5. One change can alter many things.
6. The best changes come from simply revamping the way *we* act.

Imagine what could happen in your business if you and your staff simply lived by these six principles. Erickson once said, "Rely on the capacities of the individual to furnish you the cues and the information." DeShazer likened the process to a key and a lock. A key opens a lock. Understanding the nature of the lock is not as important as having a key that fits and works.

Exceptions happen to all of us, and precisely because they are exceptions, we tend to forget or at least discount their value.

Behind the Truly Motivated

In the business sector, managers have seen that truly motivated employees and associates seem to work from an inner drive. While these workers value money, praise, and often rewards, they don't appear to depend upon them for their inner motivation. Fortunate indeed is the manager with a staff of inner directed, truly motivated workers. Solution Focused Management seeks to discover that inner ability, pattern, style of work, and problem-solving talent unique to each worker and group.

Think of what you could accomplish in your work if you were able to find the unique key that unlocks the potential of others. Think of the hours you can save when you know how to solve troubling business and personal problems.

Positive Thinking Works—For Some

One of the principles long expounded in business literature is the value of positive thinking. To think and visualize is to form and fashion the future. If my sales skills are poor, an important step in my development is to visualize my sales—and success—as I wish them to be. Becoming successful is then much more likely. In management, in financial strategy, in goal coaching, in virtually every part of every business day, the principles of positive thinking have been of great help to many. Some find it the key that unlocks their potential.

But for others, positive thinking is a source of real frustration. For these people, positive thinking doesn't unlock their potential, rather it frustrates their sincere attempts. For a discouraged sales force, a troubled work department, a confused board of directors, or a family in conflict, positive thinking is useful only *after* they harness their own courage and see the light of day within themselves.

Our research has demonstrated that Solution Focused Management taps solutions which already exist within us. This same information is inside our team, our organization, and even our families. It exists to such a degree that discouragement becomes encouragement, defeat becomes victory, and confusion becomes clarity. All this happens from the "inside out." Thus, focusing on solutions is positive. Once this principle is understood, there is no reason to focus on the problem.

> *"Take time for training."*
> —Rudolf Dreikurs
> *Have patience and show confidence in the person's ability to learn. There are no resistant learners, only inflexible teachers.*
> —Adapted from
> Michele Weiner-Davis

CHAPTER SIX

A Short Course in Solution Development

"Death is something you can do nothing about. Nothing at all. But youth is a quality, and if you have it you never lose it."

—Frank Lloyd Wright

So it is with problems. Some we can change. Some we can't. What we *can* do with both is to change us—our outlook. And our outlook can be useful or dead. It's up to us.

The Plan

In its simplest form, Solution Focused Management follows this pattern:

Step 1. *What happens?* This will be as close to the problem as you will need to get. Get a clear, concise visual picture of what's wrong, what happens, who does what to whom, and when. This visual picture need not be detailed. Think of the problem description as what Michele Weiner-Davis refers to as a home video, and you'll have all you need. Say, "If I were there, what would I see?"

Step 2. *What's it like when that doesn't happen?* Think back to a time when this complaint didn't happen. Think about even a fleeting moment when it didn't occur and describe that event. Again, in a video format, what happened? What did you see, hear, feel, etc.?

Step 3. *What are you doing when it doesn't happen?* Don't worry about others. Focus on yourself. And again get a visual (even visceral) picture of what *you* did differently in that situation when the problem wasn't a problem. This may include physically doing something different, saying something different to yourself, or appearing different to others. It might even include doing nothing instead of something, then noting what's different about that!

Step 4. *Initiate a task to do more of what you did when you didn't have the problem.* This action step, known also as *More of the Same*, allows you to notice the differences between the problem and the solution. In fact, it's often useful, when faced with a problem, to do *any* activity and then notice what happens that's different. This provides you with instant and important feedback.

An everyday family example can illustrate the thinking process that focuses on solutions first.

Step 1. A 5½-year-old boy almost always picks a fight with his father over breakfast, before the school bus arrives. No matter how the father reacts (usually in the way child rearing books suggest), the same incidents happen over and over again, and everyone in the family is discouraged. This father has a problem. So does his son.

Step 2. Once in the past 14 school days, in fact the previous Thursday, there was no fight. Briefly astounded, the father noticed it but chalked it off to luck or even to a "suspicious plan that the boy is working on!" But, despite the father's experience, one out of fourteen days went extremely well—a rare but visual and describable situation.

Step 3. Upon reflection, the father remembered that the only thing different about that Thursday morning was that, upon waking, he quietly slid into his son's bed, gently kissed him awake and spent no more than five minutes in soft whispers and quiet conversation. Then all else went the same—except there was no arguing.

Step 4. The father did more of the same. One day, another quiet talk in bed. The next, a race to see who could get dressed first. The next, a bedside puppet show. The next, five minutes of story time. And in the next fourteen days, there were only three minor arguments.

Important Learnings

This example is a simple one, but it points out the important elements of Solution Focused Management.

1. You can win another's cooperation without having to ask for it (known as the "I can only change me" rule of human relations). Here the father didn't even have to consult his son in order to win the cooperation.
2. If one person makes one small change, the whole situation can change (known as the "ripple effect"). The father changed, *then* the son and the situation automatically changed.
3. Dramatic change isn't perfection. Nothing works all the time (known as the "wish it could be" rule). It isn't necessary for your solution to work all the time.

4. The task can be varied and have the same effect (known as the "let's experiment with success" principle). Many variations of the solution strategy will probably work.

Notice what the father did here. He looked at the *situation* and *himself*. He did not look to his son. That would be problem focused. Observing the situation and himself, he became solution focused. And it worked!

Apply the same principle to your business day. What would happen if, with your most troubling problems, you focused only on what it's like when the problem isn't there or when the problem is present to a lesser degree? Imagine what you'd be doing differently that would re-create those events. Forecast what your business would then be like if you did more and more of this solution-oriented work. What do you think your team would say if you never referred to a problem again? How would they respond when, after a discussion of problems, you asked questions such as these:

- What's it like when it's not like that?

- How is that different?

- How is a small piece of it already happening?

- What effect does it have on us?

- How did we do that?

- What do we need to do to make one small step in that direction?

- What would happen if we did more of that?

- As we continue to make progress, even over the next few days, what are some indications that we're on the right track?

- What do we need to do to cause this to happen more often?

- How will we know when we are successful?

Some managers and consultants have told us this small repertoire of questions has completely changed the direction of meetings, strategies, sales presentations, and indeed even the direction of companies and careers.

Sports and Spouses Too

Let's consider the baseball player referred to in chapter three. Instead of rehashing his recent batting slump, his coach gave him videos of his *pre-slump* hitting to watch. That's what it was like when it wasn't like this! His average skyrocketed!

But what about deeper, perhaps more lasting problems, those we've always assumed were "personality problems?"

> Joe and Sue were married for twenty-one years. Over the last five to eight years, the quality of their sexual life has suffered because of their busy lives, growing children, unresolved conflicts, and a host of other stressors. They simply weren't making love very much.
>
> Upon reflection, both remembered one particular time when sex was great. The only thing different was that they talked briefly about their day while they were alone together. In fact, they were on a business trip and had tea in the hotel lobby. It happened years ago, but the moment was quite visual. As Joe off-handedly characterized it, "I guess we had to have 'verbal intercourse' before we had sexual intercourse."
>
> On a chance, both decided to talk before sex. They even tried having "verbal intercourse" before nothing at all! It worked surprisingly well—so much so that they became humorously suspicious when one said to the other, "Let's talk!"

Years of psychotherapy, attending sexual dysfunction clinics, or having extended conversations were all quite unnecessary for this couple. The solution was already there, just waiting to be remembered.

Notice what they discovered. There *was* a very real incident in their own experience that both knew had happened. They knew what had worked and that it could be repeated. With mutual cooperation and some reminiscence, they discovered what they *already knew but had forgotten*—or hadn't noticed. The end result was a mutual strategy which solved the problem.

With Uncooperative Work Partners

When you have an uncooperative partner, focus closely on Step 3: What *you* need to do differently (*not* what he or she needs to change).

Roger, an experienced salesman, prided himself on his telephone technique. In most cases, with research and persistence he was able to get through to the highest level decision maker necessary. Using correspondence, frequent calls, familiarity with the product, and a personal touch with secretarial and administrative staff, he often gained phone access and accomplished his next goal: a face-to-face appointment with that decision maker.

Using his standard repertoire of techniques, he aimed high for a particular account, a gem of a prospect. His efforts were thwarted, however, by the executive's secretary, who felt honor-bound to protect her boss. Roger persisted—all to no avail. He even used his "last ditch" technique, an impromptu office visit. His standard, "I was nearby and thought I'd take a chance," opener usually didn't work, but the visit added to his research. He learned names, assessed the atmosphere, and increased his familiarity with the company.

As he waited for the secretary to finish a phone call, Roger noticed a row of testimonials, framed letters, and plaques ringing the office walls. Most were addressed to Mr. Jones, but a few referred to him as "Butch," apparently his nickname during his Viet Nam service. When she finished the phone call, the secretary firmly, politely, and professionally dismissed Roger.

"She's the toughest I've ever met," he thought to himself. As he left the office, he heard her talking on the phone. "I'll meet you at 12:00 after my lunch substitute gets here," she said.

An old reliable technique of calling when a substitute was there often worked for Roger. A temporary worker or a member of the typing pool would take the phones for an hour or so during lunch. More discouraged than not, Roger picked up the phone over lunch, called Mr. Jones and was immediately put on hold—what seemed like eternal hold—before being transferred to the executive offices. While doodling at his desk, Roger thought of his own Viet Nam service, the guys, even the "Butches" he had known. Lost in reminiscence, the voice on the other end said, "Mr. Jones's office."

Without any forethought Roger heard himself say, "Is Butch there?" He gasped quietly as the voice quickly said, "One moment please." The next voice on the phone was Mr. Jones.

Roger inadvertently focused on himself, on what he needed to change. The resulting "key" was almost accidental. However, it was a key discovered through his persistence, research, and by doing something different. He could have been stopped at any point along the way, and he would have become discouraged.

When confronted with an uncooperative partner, don't stop what you are about to do, just focus quite clearly on yourself. The key idea here is that there are times when an uncooperative partner *is* cooperative. Even fleeting moments of cooperation are enough to get you started. But, if you focus on the other person rather than on yourself, you'll be powerless to do anything.

A furniture salesperson was checking stock for a large order of mattresses. The customer was ready to buy and short on time. When the clerk checked with the stockroom, it became clear supplies were depleted, and new shipments were too far in the future. Her anxious customer, ready to move on to another supplier, showed his irritation openly. The salesperson was aware of the ominous importance of silences. She kept a running banter going, exhausting the possibilities of stock, shipment, and price. She believed she was about to lose the order. To keep the customer, she'd have to change strategy and soon.

She looked for the "fleeting moments" of cooperation and change. She noticed that the customer relaxed "a bit" when she looked *at* him, spoke *with* him, and listened *to* him when she wasn't on the phone. Her phone banter seemed to make things worse. So she changed only her own behavior. She put down the phone and, calling it "a new game plan," looked, spoke, and listened as if her sale depended upon it—it did! She clearly noted the customer's needs and then outlined her options for servicing the order. The more she looked, spoke, and listened, the more cooperative her customer became. He obviously felt she knew his needs and was attempting to meet them.

Many sales associates in the same circumstances make excuses, engage in useless conversation, blame the inventory, or try to switch the sale to other merchandise. Sales books are full of suggestions about "handling the objections." In this case, she needed only to consult her own experience to know what would work with *this* customer. And she needed only to note those "fleeting moments" of cooperation.

Or, take an example closer to home.

When Chet saw that his wife, Mary, was preoccupied with her work, he tried to be supportive and understanding. After a month of little contact, however, he grew resentful, harsh, and openly confrontational at home. She became more entrenched, bringing work home and generally isolating herself from him. He attempted to help her manage her work and time better. He scheduled family events and socializing with friends, but to no avail.

Mary then became the resentful one. He tried to cheer her up. Nothing. Chet tried to make himself happy and just "do his own thing." Nothing.

One day, he noticed that Mary laughed in the car on the way to the store. This exception pointed the way for him. The only thing Chet could remember was making a cheery comment, really to himself, not even knowing she had heard him.

In fact, she had laughed when he carried on an imaginary conversation with a radio announcer who annoyed him when he was stuck in traffic. He noticed the laugh and noticed the circumstances. He then began the task of *having fun in front of her*, but not fun that required her to participate. Pay dirt! Mary was still preoccupied at times, but more often she was fun!

CHAPTER SEVEN

It's Not Always Easy to Identify

When problems aren't easy to identify, break them up into small, bite-sized chunks. Try not to look at the total package. In fact, this is a good rule of thumb for all solution focused work. Aim for the lowest common denominators—a day instead of a week, a subtotal rather than a grand total, even a glance rather than a conversation. John Walter and Jane Peller, Chicago-based counselors and consultants who use the solution focused model in their work, give the following example to illustrate their point:

Imagine you are pushing a stalled car. Once the car begins to move, it is much easier to maintain the forward movement. Any of us, regardless of our size, could keep the car moving with a little push. When we work from exceptions, we are using the forward movement that already exists to move the car a bit more. Noticing what is already moving, even in movement in small ways can make all the difference in the world.

With Teams

Here is another example of an elusive and difficult problem.

Five members of a Management Information Systems team were in a meeting for most of the morning, attempting to forge a consensus statement for a task force. Time was critical and the structure needed to be as precise as possible before the study could begin. After three hours of divisiveness, one solution focused thinker said meekly, "What are we like when we're not like this?" After the routine quizzical looks, one by one the ideas began to come. This was, in fact, the first time all five had met together for an important time-limited problem.

Working strictly from that suggestion, the group decided to "take breaks from the group," and build consensus with this new approach. No more than three members were allowed in the conference room at any one time. Those who were "breaking" could work alone, seek ideas outside of the room, do research, etc. The diagnosis and solution came by the end of the day.

Notice what happened here. Using a carefully phrased question focusing on a solution, this group was able to solve the problem by themselves. Quite possibly, they created a precedent for when future problems arise.

This is a kind of mental shift. Like the shift Frank Lloyd Wright made speaking of death and youth in Chapter Six, once you "have it, you never lose it."

Have the courage . . .

. . . To say no
. . . To say yes
. . . To be imperfect
. . . To be yourself
. . . And courage simply means the ability to take
one step forward.

CHAPTER EIGHT

Miracles Do Happen . . . When We Make Them Happen

"The whole point of composing is to sound inevitable."

—Aaron Copeland

Miracles

Sometimes exceptions just don't seem to happen. All people aren't so cooperative and all problems aren't so easy to identify. When there appears to be no exception, ask what would happen if a miracle occurred and what you would be doing as a result.

As a strategy for meetings and planning, this is a most useful technique. Rather than staying bogged down in the limitations of the present, the *miracle question* allows us to move into the preferred future.

A small hospital system was losing important cash because of the jumble of collection procedures used by each of its eight independent hospitals. Each was guided by different rules, priorities, and urgencies.

37

Collections were sporadic and poorly done. At a planning meeting, the system's chief financial officer posed a variation of the miracle question. He said, "What do we want to have happen by next year?" The immediate (and obvious) answer came back, "We want more money collected." He then continued, "If a miracle happened, and tomorrow there was no problem, what would we be doing differently?" The answer to this question clarified the tasks. 1) Centralize the effort; 2) staff it with specialists in collections; 3) commit for one year.

A fairly routine solution. But then the CFO added more to the miracle question. "As we begin to make progress toward this goal—even in the next few days—what are some indicators that we are on the right track?" A lively discussion about preliminary organizational efforts ensued. The CFO then said, "And what would be different?" It was during this discussion that each member of the meeting could clearly see how this attempt was really "different." In the process, each "bought into the idea" of centralizing the effort and worked together on the goal.

Precise Confrontation

The "miracle question", as deShazer refers to it, can also be used in the unlikely event that no exceptions are currently available. This technique gives us the exceptional ability to forecast our future. It also presents (confronts) us with precisely what *we* must do to change the present. For example, when there are no exceptions, you might ask, "If a miracle happened tonight, what would happen?" Again, look for a visual video image.

Early on in the relationship, it dawned on the vice-president that he had hired the wrong secretary. Though she breezed through pre-employment interviews, including one with him, she simply made too many mistakes. She was a disaster in the making. As a last-ditch effort, he searched for some exceptions but found none. If a miracle happened, he fantasized, she and he would be a finely tuned team—the kind you see pictured in those brochures for office equipment! She would be consulting with him and he with her, a cooperative partnership where work was shared. She would be his strongest asset; he'd be her best advocate. "Fat chance," he thought. But, if that miracle happened, what would *he* be doing?

He listed three things. First, he would plan his work in collaboration with her each morning. Second, he'd be at her desk, and she'd be at his, more often than now. And third, he'd be able to compliment her and tell others about her achievements. The solution search was obvious. He needed to do those things and then notice what happened. The vice-president acted "as if" his miracle had come true for two weeks. As it turned out, he made his own miracle.

The use of the "miracle question" helped get him on track. The visual image allowed him to create a new strategy for the situation. And, most important, this technique gave him a way of acting on his frustration, and put him back in charge of his own behavior.

CHAPTER NINE

Solution Focused Conflict

Rudolf Dreikurs, the late well-known Chicago psychiatrist and author, once said,

"The first step to improving the situation is the realization that we play an active part in every conflict, and that our part is the only factor we can influence. We can change no one but ourselves, but no one else's part in the conflict can remain unchanged if our part changes. The solution to any difficulty rests in our hands alone. It is useless to wait for the other fellow to take the initiative, and waiting only aggravates the matter. We can only change ourselves."

Here's an example of Dreikurs' ideas in a working situation:

One inexperienced, newly promoted manager was in conflict with a rebellious line employee. The manager wished they had more rapport, rather than the constant confrontational style which had developed. Sometimes, when the young man laughed and seemed to have fun, their rapport was better. However, this solution was unpredictable. The times when things were better didn't seem to happen with any rhyme or reason.

Then the solution became clear to the manager. She created a kind of movie for herself, a visual image of what having fun would be like. Focusing on the solution gave her the prescription: have fun, make jokes, and be as *unpredictable* with him as he was with her. She did so and he seemed better, though never completely perfect. The manager discovered the way to wisdom had been present within her and within the employee all the time.

Let's look at some specific applications of this model in areas of every day business management: coaching, conflict resolution, and in Chapter Eleven, collaboration.

Coaching Your Staff and Yourself

What would happen the next time a member of your team came to you for help, and you focused on the solution rather than the problem? After the initial complaint, you might say, "What is it like when it's not like that?" In addition to a quizzical look, many people respond with a quiet, searching expression. Indeed! They *are* searching. They're searching for *exceptions to the problem*—the foundation of solutions.

Or, after the initial description of the complaint, you may say, "Suppose a miracle happened tonight, and tomorrow this problem was gone. What would be different?"

In either case, the manager then focuses full-time on the exceptions or the differences. Questions such as "How did you do that?" or "How were you able to decide to cooperate in that way?" or "How were you able to plan so quickly?" are all appropriate queries to help the person focus on solutions.

"Give me a fish and I eat for a day; teach me to fish and I'll eat for a lifetime" is an appropriate age-old saying for the solution focused manager. Employees will be empowered not only by what they can do, but by the knowledge of what they've already done to make the difference.

This one skill is an invaluable aid for managers doing any kind of coaching. It's encouraging, easy to use, and consistent with research in counseling theory and personality development.

Conflict Resolution

When conflict arises, you can apply the same principles of solution focused thinking. Take this recent case of a secretary complaining about his boss to another secretary.

Linda: You seemed pretty angry after the staff meeting today.

George: I hate the way he makes decisions lately.

Linda: The budget?

George: I guess. It's more the way he treats me about it.

Linda: (Nodding)

George: 'Just wish I could cope better. I know *he* isn't going to change.

Linda: So if you could solve it, or better yet (chuckling) if a miracle happened tonight, and *you were able to cope better*, what would you be doing differently?

George: I guess I wouldn't take it so personally.

Linda: When you don't take it so personally, what are *you* doing?

George: Last week he messed me up on one of the budget revisions, but I had so much to do I just kept working.

Linda: And, what happened?

George: Everything went fine.

Linda: So what did you do?

George: I kept working anyway. I had so much to do, I just didn't think about it much.

Linda: And that worked . . . I mean it helped you to cope better?

George: (Intrigued) He and I went head-to-head about the Christmas schedule two weeks ago. I let him have it. I've never been that direct with him before. I wasn't so composed on the inside though!

Linda: And? What happened?

George: It was fine, he listened. In a funny way, it seemed almost as if he respected me more!

Linda: How did you decide to "go head-to-head"?

George: I don't know.

Linda: And being more direct helped, even though it was hard to do?

George: It really made all the difference in the world—yes!

Linda: So when you're able to cope better, what seems as if it will work best for you?

George: I guess I could either just keep on working or be more direct. It did work before didn't it?

Notice what Linda did here. First, the focus was only on what George stated as the goal ("to cope better"). Linda didn't give advice; she didn't give opinions about the boss, the meeting, or the budget. Linda didn't even talk about any of the details. The only focus was on when George had coped better, a time George had forgotten.

Second, Linda encouraged George to be responsible for self-change ("how did you decide . . . "). This subtle, but most important encouragement skill again keeps the focus clearly where it belongs: on George and his very real ability to solve his own problem.

Third, focusing on solutions avoids the often repetitious and frustrating historical (and hysterical!) details about the other person. Frank Walton, a South Carolina psychologist, has said that in most conflicts, we are all too well aware of what the other person needs to change. "That," says Walton, "is about the most useless information we can have!" And often we are tempted to focus on a kind of "useless talk."

CHAPTER TEN

Even "Junk" Works

Focusing on your own change works at home, too.

Laura, the mother of four teenage girls, had a problem. She wanted to have at least some meals together as a family, the way they once did. But in her busy household everyone seemed to go his or her own way. Laura attempted to cook big dinners, but little happened. A recovering cancer patient herself, she went to great lengths to keep healthful food available and to ban "junk food."

Without being aware of it, her health-orientation made the problem worse. No one was rushing to the table for broccoli! The more she focused on her daughters and her husband, the worse her nagging became. Their absences from the dinner table produced mutual discouragement; family frustration increased.

One Sunday she prepared an elaborate dinner, with written invitations formally asking all to attend. She intrigued them. When they walked into the dining room, a spectacular "junk food dinner" awaited. Popcorn, chips, cheese dip, candy in abundance, soft drinks, and half a dozen other delights—even a carefully arranged centerpiece made of those famous creme filled cakes! What followed was a rollicking two-hour family dinner the likes of which would rival a Leo Buscaglia story! Mom did what she could do; she ceased worrying about what the rest of the family would do.

This family now rotates meal preparation and has one special dinner per week—"green dinners" (everything served must be green), "fiesta night" (Mexican food), "round evenings" (lots of circular food). Their imaginations have run wild with the possibilities. In addition to *seizing the initiative*, a most critical conflict resolution skill, this very determined mother did what she thought she had to do that was quite different from what her family expected her to do!

These two complementary, but very different, approaches focus on solutions; they don't focus on problems. Imagine what you could do with sticky problems, those of others or your own, by simply following Laura's example.

CHAPTER ELEVEN

Collaboration

As a group works together, it's helpful to notice when rapport builds, when consensus happens, and when productivity occurs. When groups don't work well together, or when they hit a sticky point, it's useful to recall the "working times." The previously mentioned question, "What were we like when we weren't like this?", can get the group back on track quickly and easily.

Boards of directors, work teams, contract negotiators, advisory councils, and other groups can use this simple technique to stay on task. A solution focused manager can add encouragement in both subtle and substantial ways by focusing on the solution.

One manager of a successful real estate firm was always impressed by the cooperation that existed among her staff. All were independent contractors. These commission-only "lone wolves" worked side-by-side with very little difficulty. In a highly competitive profession, she was further impressed by how the successful salespeople valued customers, time, and money. Although each was known to be somewhat "cut-throat" when necessary, she was thankful it didn't happen in the office with each other.

As manager, her day-to-day responsibility was as a resource person and advisor to the staff, a go-between for the owner of the company, and the overseer of materials and supplies. One quasi-official duty was mediating disputes. Since these disputes didn't happen very often, she was glad this was one hat she could keep in storage! Until that one day!

Two of the manager's best producers had an argument over a referral fee for a customer who seemed to belong to both of them. The disagreement was over $800.00. Pride was at stake too. They brought the details to the mediator for her decision. Being no-nonsense types, they wanted to know who was going to get what.

This Solomon-like dilemma placed the manager at great risk. With independent people, any decision that wasn't self-generated was likely to hold little weight.

By thinking about "what are they like when they aren't like this," she came upon a solution. She asked both to accompany her to the conference room bringing all of the materials pertinent to their case. Once inside, she said the following:

"You are both top producers. You work well together, and each one of you values your customers, your time, and your money. I have great respect for each of you. Therefore, I trust your mutual judgment on this matter. I want you to work it out. When you have a mutually agreed upon solution to your problem, let me know. In the meantime, as your facilitator and mediator, I'll take all your phone messages, I'll bring in your dinner and your breakfast if necessary. I'll keep everyone else out of your way. When you have an agreement, let me know."

She walked out, placed a prominent "Do Not Disturb" sign on the door, sat in front of the conference room, and continued with her paperwork. Within an hour, the agreement was struck. She reviewed it and took both associates out to dinner!

By allowing solutions to be our focus, we can help more people faster. And in doing so, we help them help themselves.

The manager knew that in this case the only solution had to come from the two salespersons, not from her. She knew her people better than they knew themselves. She harnessed all of their inner motivation and then *got out of the way*. This is sound advice for any manager.

Specific applications to business are abundant. In counseling, conflict resolution, collaboration, or in any area that involves others or change, Solution Focused Management and solution focused thinking can be a breath of fresh air.

CHAPTER TWELVE

To Begin

"What forms the character of a human being?
. . . (we depend) on the cooperation of others."
—Rudolf Dreikurs

As you implement this model, we suggest you adapt it to your current methods, rather than adopting it wholeheartedly at once. Remember, as a manager your most important "tool" is you. *How* you use *what* you use is important, but *who you are* is the critical element of healthy, useful, and productive relationships with others.

As you incorporate new methods or skills in your work, do so gradually. In this way, it will truly become your own. Your comfort with this new method will give it life and appeal.

In the coming chapters, you'll learn the specifics of how to integrate this new learning into your own particular style. Proceed in keeping with the theory, "look for small beginnings and small changes".

New ideas do feel odd at first—clumsy and uncomfortable. It *is* easier to do it the old way. We encourage you to risk discomfort. There are countless opportunities in a business or family to do something slightly different. In this way, you can keep growing, sharpen your skills, and even find out what doesn't work. Our experience demonstrates that you will also discover a rich storehouse of what does work. Those you work with will be richer and more productive for their contact with you.

Review

Now it's time to review these first chapters and use what you've learned both on the job and at home.

Thus far you've discovered:

- The problem with problems . . . knowing more about the problem does not always lead to the solution. In fact, "problem talk" can take you in the wrong direction entirely.

- The silent solutions already within you, your family, your work team. You need look no further for practical solutions because they exist inside of you.

- Specific things to say to elicit cooperation from others, a script that works in many situations.

- What to do when you hit the brick wall of discouragement and defeat. What was one concrete idea that literally put you on the road to reversing your worst setback?

- A new way of thinking that doesn't require you to change your personality . . . only your way of approaching solutions.

- Ideas for your next conflict, and techniques you can use immediately.

- Ways to monitor the progress of your next task.

- Even a new method to make small talk on your next business trip. "What's it like when it's not like that?" is a sure attention getter!

To Do

Use this Section to jot down some notes. Review our Review, then circle one or two (at the most three) ideas that seem the easiest and most natural for you to implement today, tomorrow, the day after, and into next week. Work on these "small beginnings." Notice what was different or better.

- *Become "problem-free."* Drop the word "problem" from your everyday vocabulary. Literally, don't say it anymore. See how often you can sidestep your own use of the word "problem." Look for alternatives like "challenge" or "opportunity."

- *DSD—"Do Something Different."* Do slight, small things differently, especially in that part of your day which may be the most routine.

- When you notice change happening as a result of doing something different, then *DMS—"Do More of the Same."* Doing More of the Same helps maintain the environment for productivity. It also keeps you from trying to mess up your success in the name of creativity. Allow what works to work!

- *Look for "exceptions"* in your own behavior and notice what's happening at those times. Observe what is different.

- At meetings or one-on-one, ask, *"What's it like when it's not like that?"*

- When you are really stumped, discouraged, or defeated, ask yourself, *"If a miracle happened tonight and I didn't have this problem, what would be different?"*

- Next time you're in a conflict, *be unpredictable.* Turn 180 degrees from your normal response. Then notice what is different.

- When people come to you for advice, quietly resist giving it. Instead, focus full-time on their *"exceptional moments."*

- *Focus on others' natural strengths.* Intersperse your normal conversation at home, while commuting, at work, etc., with comments such as, "How did you decide to do that?" or, "Is it different for you to do it in that way?" or, "Did others seem to notice the difference?"

- In group situations, such as when coaching your children's teams or arguing with your spouse, ask, "What was it like when it wasn't like this?" or, "What were we doing when it wasn't like this?"

- And, as you begin to make *any progress* toward a goal, *review* the essential ingredients. "As we continue to make progress, what are more small indicators that we are on the right track?" and, "What do we need to continue to do more of that?"

A Personal Note

Our experience with solution focused managers has convinced us that there are many different people and managers who can use these techniques and that they need not change their personalities or leadership style to do so. The tools of Solution Focused Management are simply additional resources for your collection. We suggest you treat them as such—*additions* to your already existing repertoire.

For some managers, these tools replace older technology. Others become especially adept at using the tools in specific situations. And for still others, these techniques transform the way they do business, the way they live, the way they influence people, even the way they raise their children. But conversion isn't necessary. In your case it may not even be desirable. Use what works for you.

> *Stay out of fights.*
>
> *One can, and should, have a friendly discussion about fighting, without the least hint of finger-pointing or of moralizing, and work out the ways and means of settling difficulties. However, this cannot be done while the fight is taking place; for at this point, words do not "teach" or "help"—they merely become additional weapons in the fight already in progress.*
>
> —Dreikurs and Soltz

CHAPTER THIRTEEN

From Conflict to Cooperation

"The only way out is through."

—C. S. Lewis

In Vienna, during the late 1800s, a custom developed to "initiate" newly married couples. After the wedding, but before the reception, the guests took the young couple to the woods behind the chapel. Once there, they were given a bucksaw, a tool with two handles used by lumberjacks to cut down trees. A tree was selected, and the couple were instructed to cut it down with the bucksaw. The newlyweds struggled with the task until the tree fell. Then the older women would huddle and speculate about how long this new marriage would last.

—Retold by Rudolf Dreikurs

In the late 1800s, Alfred Adler, a Viennese psychiatrist, once remarked that love was desirable but was not necessary for the success of a marriage. Calling marriage "a task for two," he said cooperation was more important than love.

Today, at home and at work, we've discovered cooperation—not good intention—is *the* requirement of successful relationships. Rudolf Dreikurs, Adler's disciple in America in the mid 1900s, said, "We can't require cooperation-we can only win it."

Managers know, sometimes through the most bitter of experiences, that cooperation can never be required. Active management is a task, a task for two. Like the bucksaw, active management requires pacing, work, energy, and timing—all in a unique choreography which depends on both the partners and the task.

Conflict, like cooperation, is also a task for two. This relationship factor—that most of what happens occurs *between* people—is a key ingredient in all of our dealings with one another.

For the solution focused manager, this is the one bright spot in conflict process. Since conflict and cooperation happen between people, we can, rightly oriented, influence the other person simply by changing ourselves. For when we change ourselves, we've changed the interaction. Then, by natural process, the partner will have the opportunity to change.

A real issue for leaders is, "What do I do when . . . ?" Management experience teaches that there are few "pat" answers to any situation. A blending of elements of the management role—its skills, its crafts, its act—still remains the most graceful of arts.

Principle #1: Focus on the interaction, not the person.

When properly focused on the interaction, the manager has wide latitude. There's an absence of competition. Focusing on interaction is more likely to lead to a sense of cooperation, i.e. working with others on a common task.

In short, this kind of focus will work only when you look to those things over which you have control. We can't truly manipulate another person, but we can have great impact over our own part of the interaction with that person. Such self-change will influence change in the other person.

Of course, not everyone we experience conflict with will have the same view.

"My boss rules by intimidation. He thinks that to ensure our monthly quota, he needs to brow-beat us, threaten to transfer us to different territories, fire us, and worse!

I always reach my quota and beyond because of my inner drive and because I'm fair and supportive of my people. But when I go to the weekly supervisors' meetings, he consistently yells, screams, and rules! My boss's boss is no help. As long as a quota is met, he looks the other way.

This is not a healthy environment. What can I do?"

When we focus on the intimidator, the yells, the screams, even the looking the other way, we put ourselves in a very frustrating position. The simple truth is that even the boss's boss is helpless to control any of these items.

However, by focusing on the interaction (How is he with *me*? How am *I* with him?) we are more likely to notice progress.

After a Solution Focused Management consultation, the manager continued.

"Because my performance and my quota numbers were above average, I didn't really have a problem with my boss personally. But the unhealthy environment was very discouraging. I used to try to sit silently during the meetings as much as I could. But, after this Solution Focused Management meeting, I noticed that the few times I did talk, my boss listened quietly and usually nodded in agreement. What's more, that sparked spontaneous discussion with the others in attendance. At least until my boss screwed it up with more yelling!

"So, I tried a new tactic. Rather than being a receiver, I decided to be a translator between my boss and the others. I decided to act *as if* my boss's yelling was his frustration level and was an implicit invitation for me to reinterpret and translate his frustration into more understandable language. As long as he nodded, and as long as they talked, I knew I was on the right track. (And I was safe too!)"

Principle #2: Don't listen to words, watch the feet.

The world of work is sometimes the world of words. And words can easily fail us. Explanations, suggestions, rationalizations, progress reports, humor, and dozens of other kinds of word-filled interactions, don't always amount to much. Except maybe more confusion. When we "listen too much," we literally take in too much data. The result? We overload and confuse ourselves and others.

As a manager, it's important to know and do. The manager's role is to guide, develop, and be the compass for the employees and team.

As one health care manager said to us in a Solution Focused Management consultation session, "I know my boss hasn't got the slightest idea of how I do what I do. But I know when I get lost or stuck, she knows where I should go next. That's the mystery for me. How does she know that?"

Words and explanations can be circular and nondirectional, but feet always point in the direction they are going. Keeping the end goal in alignment with the "feet" of the team is another management task. Managers who spend too much time on the details of a project will find that they, too, may tend to feel adrift occasionally because they have lost their unique position and their special vantage point.

"My department is a mix of age groups. Some people have been with the company twenty to twenty-five years, and some for only a year or two. I am younger than the majority of the people, and though I have been with the company for only a few years, I was recently named supervisor of the whole office. How do I keep these people motivated and productive, keeping in mind the differences in ages, education levels, perspectives about the company, jobs, and about me as their new supervisor?"

This manager could easily believe the more she knows about each person the better. On the contrary, we think that emphasis would be an error. It could be data overload. Her job is to keep a keen eye on the goal, and be sure to reinterpret the goal through the unique set of experiences and skills of each of her team. By doing this, she will find her people to be more directional and less likely to divide over their differences.

What the manager focuses on will be precisely what the team focuses on. For this reason, the manager must set her sights on seeing a clearly stated and realistic goal. Too much clutter will confuse and discourage her team.

As for differences in age, education, and tenure, keep in mind that to get where you are going, it matters less the kind or condition of your shoes, than which way you keep your feet pointed.

Therefore, this manager would be better off to watch as her staff makes progress towards the goal. As she notices how each team member moves toward the goal, she will have a rich storehouse of data that works.

Principle #3: Resist the first impulse.

"Our sales region has been floundering. The new CEO, the fourth in the past two years, decides to slip into town to observe a quarterly sales meeting. She sees a number of the sales force drunk, not only for the meeting but also for the reporting session. She observes that they brag to each other about the seemingly underhanded way in which they got their sales. This CEO believes in personal and company integrity, hard work, and a strong sense of ethics. She wants to turn this situation around."

In *Alice in Wonderland*, the Queen of Hearts is well-known for the phrase, "Off with their heads." Some corporate managers use this approach too. But we think it is flawed. It focuses on the person and not the interaction, and it pays too much attention to words.

To turn the situation around, this CEO can employ another technique to guide her thinking.

Principle #4: Take time for training.

This sales meeting may be a microcosm of the larger corporate behavior. But it might also be a symptom of another problem, namely that of ignorance. The CEO decided on this plan of attack:

1. She resisted her first impulse to fire or discipline anyone immediately. This would have sidetracked the survivors from the real goal and reflected poorly on the CEO.
2. Through extensive consultation with all levels, she forged a new goal statement that everyone agreed with.
3. She initiated a training program combining capitalism and ethics. Through seminars, consultation, and strategy meetings, the CEO fixed her eye on the long-range goal of having a successful, ethical sales staff—and she took the time to train them.
4. Sales meetings were distinguished from sales celebrations. The latter had an open bar, but only for a half-hour. The former was held on a work day with lots of coffee available.

The results? Within six months those who couldn't produce under the new management chopped their own heads, while those who could, found a place for training, productivity and reward.

Resisting the first impulse is not easy. Counting to ten when we're angry is often not enough to make a tangible difference. The two techniques may seem similar. Resisting the first impulse, though, has more to do with a total management strategy than counting to ten. When we resist the first impulse, we are working with an understanding that cooperation has to be won, that what we do will make an important difference for the other person. We also realize that when we force ourselves to work under unnecessary pressure, we're likely to lose our own control.

CHAPTER FOURTEEN

The Role of Feelings

"It's easier to act your way to a new feeling than to feel your way to a new action."
—John Burton

It is much the same with our emotions. Often seen as *complicating* conflict, we now know emotions are indicators and motivators for us. Rudolf Dreikurs said emotions are to the person what gas is to the car. They fuel us. They move us. They provide the energy we then decide to tap. The key to effective conflict resolution is to understand the role of emotions in our lives.

Simply put, there are three things we can do with our emotions:

1. *We can act the way we feel.* People tend to act out their negative emotions, rather than their positive ones, without much thought of consequence. This approach is not always the most socially acceptable. It gives control to our feelings at exactly the moment they are probably at their most irrational level.

2. *We can make other people act the way we feel.* We can change the emotional climate of the office from the moment we walk in. So can everyone else. A teacher who walks into a classroom and says, "Shut up and sit down," will immediately set the tone for that class. Some teachers don't even need to say it, they just "look" it. Some managers too! The old adage is true; misery not only loves company, it demands it. When we're miserable, the only thing that makes us less miserable is making someone else miserable. You may have noticed that some of the most challenging people in your life are those who are similar to your personality. Your children who are like you are the ones you may clash with the most. Or, when you clash with them, the intensity is profoundly more difficult . . . and louder! Therefore, it's imperative to remain in control.

3. *We can realize that we can't help how we feel, but we can help how we act.* Emotions are neither right nor wrong; they just are.

Of the 243 possible common "feeling" words in our everyday English vocabulary, each can be placed under one of five major feelings: sad, mad, glad, scared, or hurt. Therefore, as a manager, it is helpful to simplify your own feelings as well as those of others by using a simple system to clarify the feelings.

"Joe, you sound mad, is that correct?"

"Martha is hurt and I feel . . . "

"Ralph, I'm glad we are . . . "

"Joe, to me you seem mad, or maybe sad. Which is right?"

Clarifying feelings is the single most helpful step toward clarifying what needs to be done in a conflict. Alfred Adler stated that although feelings provide the fuel, they don't provide the direction. Clear thinking and careful preparation do that.

When dealing with feelings and emotions work to do the following:

- *Show Respect* . . . Take all feelings seriously even if you don't understand them completely. Avoid jokes and frivolous clichés. You can use humor *gently* to receive the tension, but show you respect the person and the feeling.
- *Demonstrate Concern* . . . Eye contact, time, and a sensitive vocabulary can go a long way to help show that you care.
- *Encourage Dialogue* . . . Share your feelings, interrupt with empathy and questions, repeat and reflect what you are hearing from them. Let them know you are there!
- *Stay Professional* . . . Keep to your own common sense guidelines for that important yet invisible "line" between work and personal, professional and lay, too many details and enough to help. Act as a concerned fellow worker, not as a therapist or psychologist.
- *Listening is the Task at Hand* . . . and listening will also help *them* to solve the problem themselves.

CHAPTER FIFTEEN

Cooperation Is Inevitable (If We See It That Way)

"Cooperation isn't getting people to do what you want them to do, it's getting them to want to do what you want them to do."

—Earl Nightingale

In our work we find it useful to believe there is no such thing as resistant workers, only inflexible managers. Workers who appear to resist the work may only be resisting our interactions with them, and that resistance is more properly understood as communication. This communication may help us understand how they, in fact, *want to cooperate.*

A night supervisor, Harold, was having a difficult time getting one of his janitorial staff to follow the prescribed routine. No matter how specific his reminders, this janitor seemed determined to resist the routine. The more the supervisor persisted, the more entrenched the janitor became. Or so it seemed.

One evening Harold took the employee aside and said: "You know, Bud, I've made an error in the past few weeks. I've been under the assumption our company routine works better than yours. But I think you've been telling me the opposite. How is it that yours seems to work better for you?" The employee was taken off guard and fumbled a bit. Then, sensing the manager was "on the level," he took a chance and said, "I just work better when I do it my way." The supervisor grinned and nodded. "I had that impression, Bud. While I have you here, can I get some of your other ideas about how you'd solve the problem that we've had in the cafeteria?"

By assuming cooperation, Harold was able to reframe what looked like rebellion into a cooperative activity.

All people want:

- to belong
- to feel significant
- to have a unique identity

Skilled managers who can tap these three "wants" will find a rich resource indeed.

Who taps that in you?

Stay close to them!

CHAPTER SIXTEEN

Before All Else Fails—DSD

Along with the belief that in any situation we can only change ourselves, it helps to know what to do and what not to do. When problems recur, we often keep doing what we always did, even if it never worked!

Imagine the difference in your work place if your most violated rules were dealt with in new ways. Long lunches, excessive absences, personal days, even theft, are costly for big and small businesses alike. Even in labor negotiations, much of the work is in forecasting what the other side will or won't do. Pat answers have become so routine they are predictable. Therefore, they lose their effectiveness. On the other hand, if doing the same thing doesn't work, *doing something different* might allow for new and productive possibilities.

Great leadership may depend on this principle more than any other maxim. Military strategy, marketing direction, takeover targets, even our favorite commercials, often rely on difference—the element of surprise—rather than sameness to make a point. In the workplace, doing something different can be the beginning of creativity—new ways to do new things . . . and old things too!

Doing something different can be a logical thought process or simply a spontaneous, random, even illogical response. A careful, studied approach is not necessarily important. The crucial factor here is simply the "different-ness" of the response. And remember to work for the lowest common denominator. Smaller *is* better.

Those who appear to be naturally creative are often people who "see things differently" than their peers. Creative people look in a new way, from a different vantage point, or with a greater intensity. They literally see it differently from other people. When it comes to conflict and coopera-tion, "do something different" is a process that can be used even by the most seemingly noncreative among us.

We aren't completely sure why this approach works so well. It may be that the cycle is interrupted, or the expecta-tions are challenged, or even that when taken "off guard," people respond in newer, more constructive ways.

Notice we are not advocating *thinking* something differ-ent. Thinking doesn't move us into action. Only when we are moved to action do we really influence relationships between people. Good communication is often lost when we think rather than talk, consider rather than do, live in the abstract rather than in the concrete here and now.

What could you do today that would be different?

CHAPTER SEVENTEEN

Sometimes Don't Do Anything

Sometimes not doing anything works well also. Times when it is better not to do anything might include:

- Periods of intense conflict.

- When the other person has "really lost it."

- When you are feeling pressured to do something you know is wrong.

- When you're just so confused, so overwrought, so weary that you know any decision will be an inferior one.

Make no mistake here. Not doing anything is doing something! The something you are doing is borne of a concrete decision: the decision not to do. This decision is quite different from the indecision of doing nothing. This is a non-decision, a kind of management limbo of fear and inaction. Next time you have an opportunity to decide *not* to do, notice how it makes the situation better or different, even if only in a small way. Again, look for small changes in small ways . . . and keep noticing what happens. In doing so, you'll neutralize fear.

Fear can wipe out our initiative and our courage. Alfred Adler said that if he could give a child one personality characteristic, it would be courage. With courage, we can overcome that fear and meet the challenges before us. Not doing anything is the gentle art of quiet courage.

Certainly an advantage to using any of these strategies is that we have an opportunity to act in a new way, to have a new road to travel. Certainly we'll sense a bit more control. That sense of inner control will help us in any conflict. Doing what *we* can do, rather than waiting for what the other person may do, is the single best piece of advice we can follow in any conflict.

To further reduce fear try:

- *Exaggerating it* . . . to comic proportions!

- *Picturing it* . . . then throw the masterpiece out!

- *Planning for it* . . . later tonight (for ten minutes), or later in your life!

- *Taking it with you* . . . But keep it out of sight!

- *Admitting to it* . . . and, then, get on with your life!

CHAPTER EIGHTEEN

An Additional
Strategy—DTO

"Avoid the first impulse—do the unexpected."
—Rudolf Dreikurs

Additional strategies can help in specific situations. Our clients have told us that during times of enormous stress, just when they most need to do something different, they lose enough perspective that they literally don't know what's different. At these times, we recommend DTO—Do the Opposite. We may not know what's different, but we will know what is the opposite.

Want to yell? Whisper!

Want to punish? Forgive!

Want to be right? Say the four magic words, *"You* might be right!"

Want to intimidate? Sit down!

Want to fight? Go to the bathroom!

The genius of Dreikurs's advice is that it breaks the cycle of destructive interaction clearly and quickly. It takes any opponent off guard, keeps them guessing, buys you time, leaves no permanent mark, and gives each person a new perspective.

This is a particularly good tactic to practice on strangers and salesclerks. Most likely you'll never see them again *and* you will have the internal knowledge of how *you* changed.

A suggestion: When it comes to helping yourself change, do it in small doses.

Sit in a different chair.

Set a time limit for visitors.

Close your door more frequently (or less frequently).

Pencil in an encouraging note on a memo and return it to the sender.

Smile.

An Episcopalian Benedictine contemplative monk used this technique quite successfully. Faced with having to spend 1.2 million dollars on capital improvements for his abbey, he felt pressured as never before. He was a detail-oriented person, but he just wasn't grasping the concepts well enough to feel comfortable with the myriad of contractors involved.

Pushed to sign contracts he didn't understand, he began to sign letters of agreement instead. His letter of agreement stated his questions and directed the contractor to teach him the details. Once he mastered a rudimentary understanding of the work to be done, the agreement said that he would sign the necessary contract to begin the work. He received a number of "crash courses" in plumbing, masonry, electricity, and finance. When he felt better, he contracted. He "DS-bnmos." He did something, but not much of something!

CHAPTER NINETEEN

Person to Person Corollaries

" . . . We are in this together, and . . . together each of us can develop self-reliance as well as cooperation with others."
—Michael Popkin

When we choose a vacation destination, we are clearly focused on a goal: usually a city, a region, or a set of experiences. We look forward to the future. We pursue our goals.

So it is with our inner lives. As Dreikurs and Popkin have written, we each pursue a psychological goal. Each of us wants:

- Contact with others.

- Power and influence over our environment.

- Protection from being vulnerable.

- Privacy to be ourselves and to be with ourselves.

There are *useful* ways to pursue these goals:

- Recognition

- Independence
- Assertiveness
- Centering

And there are socially *useless* goals as well. Trouble happens when we pursue these socially useless goals:

- Undue attention seeking
- Rebellion
- Revenge
- Avoidance

People employ socially useful or socially useless goals in order to belong. It's not coincidental that our actions have a social impact on one another. This is especially true when others "misbehave" with us. Then we feel:

- Annoyed
- Angry
- Hurt
- Helpless

But there are strategies we can use to help:

A.　Be predictable about giving attention unpredictably.

B.　Sidestep the struggle for power.

C.　Take nothing personally, but seek to mend another's hurt.

D.　Never pity; encourage instead.

When you deal with people, be aware of the relationship and the goal. This will help you do those things which will have a positive impact, and refrain from doing those which will not.

Learning to understand what can be the somewhat hidden messages others send us is a great managerial advantage.

Often we can recognize those messages to us by consulting our inner feelings. Then we can design a response that fits our needs.

When we're *annoyed* with our co-workers, is it possible that what they want from us is recognition and attention? For these people, any attention—positive or negative—is better than no attention at all. In fact, it is precisely what they need to perform at their peak. Yet, in their bid to get what *they* want, we're often put off and distanced. **Corollary A** works best here. *Be predictable about giving attention unpredictably.*

If you find yourself "cornered" by the office bore, try inviting him or her out to lunch—unexpectedly. If your corporate rival is making life unpleasant for you, drop by her office and just chat—unexpectedly. When an employee is giving you the cold shoulder after a disappointing performance appraisal, collaborate with that person, one-on-one. Ask questions, ask for advice, offer encouragement—unexpectedly. And when that pushy salesperson is pitching to you just one more time, call a meeting of everyone who might use the product. Give the salesperson ten minutes on the agenda, then have everyone make a decision. And do it unexpectedly.

When we're *angry* with others, is it possible they feel they count only when they have power and influence? This power struggle can go on for a very long time, unless we know this secret: That's **Corollary B**: *Side-step the struggle for power.* Don't fight. Don't give in. Just literally don't show up for the fight. Some managers sidestep the struggle for power in the following ways:

Indirectly: Simply don't show up. You might go to the bathroom at the time of intense struggle.

Directly:	Say, "I disagree with you, George, but I want to know more about what you think."
Humorously:	"You're good! Up until now, only my spouse and my car could make me this angry!"
Seriously:	"Let's look at how we disagree, Beverly, before we go at it. Let me tell you what I think you think, and you tell me what you think I think. Then we can more precisely get to a resolution."

Many responses are possible here, but the *crucial* secret for dealing with the power struggle is to resist the temptation to fight back, put the other down, or take a superior position.

Corollary C: *Take nothing personally, but seek to mend another's hurt*. When we're hurt by what another has done to us, is it possible the other person has been inadvertently hurt by us? The desire to "even the score" will continue the conflict. Only when we refuse to be hurt and simultaneously recognize the other person's discomfort do we diffuse the conflict and address the real problem.

A sympathetic ear can go a long way in such a situation. He or she doesn't want to hear, "You shouldn't feel that way," "tomorrow will be better," or "It's history." What a hurt person wants to hear is something like, "I'm sorry if what I said or did hurt you. That wasn't my intention. Can we talk a bit more so we can straighten this out?"

Refuse to be hurt yourself, however, no matter what is said to you. And don't fight. That will only inflame the situation.

Bill:	Marge, I can see you are deeply hurt.
Marge:	Hurt? You do this to people *all* the time!
Bill:	Well, I certainly didn't mean to hurt *you*. How can I make it better?
Marge:	*Everyone* says when you blow, watch out.

Bill: You are my concern now, Marge.

Marge: It just didn't seem fair.

Bill: You might be right.

Corollary D: *Never pity, encourage instead.* When we want to give up because we feel so frustrated with the seeming inadequacy of other people, we need to subtly coach, not cajole; encourage, not criticize; develop, not diagnose. Encouragement over time works to help truly discouraged people see themselves in a new way. Short-range goals, specific objectives, conservatively positive encouragement, and task-based compliments are all part of a regimen that combats the assumed disability these people feel.

Psychologist Michael Popkin recommends that we encourage by:

1. Showing confidence in other people:

   - Give responsibility and let them know you believe they can handle it.
   - Ask for their opinions, feedback and advice.
   - Avoid the natural temptation to rescue other people and to take over.
   - Resist becoming an answer person . . . encourage, but let them figure it out.

2. Building on strengths:

   - Acknowledge what was done well.
   - Give credit for strengths (even when used somewhat inappropriately).
   - Concentrate on improvement, not perfection.
   - Give positive strokes with each step.
   - Avoid personality labels.

3. Valuing others (as they are):

- Separate their worth as people from their accomplishments as workers.
- Separate their worth as people from their mistakes.
- Appreciate each person's unique contribution (however slight it may be at the moment).

4. Stimulating independence:

- Let people do for themselves those things which they can do (even if they protest or find it difficult at first).
- Foster a sense of interdependence. Help people see their value to *each other* and to the work at hand.

CHAPTER TWENTY

Three Helpful Reminders

1. Small changes lead to larger and bigger changes.
2. The solution is probably already happening.
3. Use the metaphor.

Complete solutions—those that form a nice, neat package—happen in two main ways: in our textbooks and in our memories. They just don't occur often in real life. But while we are immersed in a conflict or a problem, this expectation can weigh heavily on us. We feel we ought to be more in control, more in charge, use more foresight, and stay calmer. Our expectation is that we ought to be able to traverse this new territory as though we'd been there before. Yet we can't expect that of ourselves. Each new territory poses its own unique challenges for us.

When we examine what really happens to problems and conflicts, we find they are best solved one step at a time. Small changes lead to bigger changes. Seemingly insignificant moves are later seen as significant ones.

One food service manager reported that her whole approach to management changed with one small piece of advice her CEO gave her in passing one day. "We're all probably just doing the best we can," he said. "We'll do better when we know better." Armed with that small concept, she engaged in what she later called an "educated management" style of her own. She very simply acted *as if* her staff just needed to know more in order to do more. She became a teacher, a tutor, a mentor to her people. It suited her and them.

Another VP in a health service organization told us that change happened regularly for him when he became aware the Alcoholics Anonymous motto of "One Day at a Time" would lead to substantive change.

Still another newly appointed manager, whose training was in engineering, simply decided to adapt some advice he had heard a prolific author explain on a radio talk show. This author, with over 100 published books in his lifetime, was asked by the interviewer, "How are you able to write so many books?" Cooley, the author replied, "Four pages a day." Our technical manager decided to read four pages a day and talk to four staff members per day. His analytical training and this systematic approach came in handy to help him adjust successfully to this much less defined art of management.

A belief that small leads to big, that individual steps lead to entire journeys, is an important feature for the solution focused manager's thinking. It will greatly influence the way we deal with each day, each issue, each person.

What small change in your experience has led to substantive change when applied to work? What small change might help reposition you even today?

It's Happening

The second helpful reminder is the fact that solutions are often already happening even though we don't always notice them.

In our attempt to solve problems, we often stumble upon solutions. These are circumstances and interruptions which solve the problem, but because they *appear* transitory or illogical, we regard them as flukes or as happenstance. In effect, they are solutions waiting to be recognized as such.

Ralph was a newly appointed supervisor in the MIS Department. As is often the case with computer departments, his promotion had more to do with his technical knowledge than with his managerial experience or expertise. He was doing well, but was plagued with one major problem. His key programmer was an independent, spirited, brilliant young woman who worked best alone. She was not a team player. Whether his interactions were with regard to decisions, data, or delays, Ralph was consistently frustrated with her isolation and what appeared to be her uncooperative attitude. At key strategy meetings, in work groups, and at reporting sessions, he was most distressed. The only times he felt her cooperation were when he would have private, one-on-one meetings with her—or even better the times when he stopped by her desk for an informal "chat."

At this point, Ralph could have easily come to the conclusion that, although his programmer worked well alone and in one-on-one, her lack of cooperation with the team put her job in jeopardy. However, the solution was already at work with his chats.

Ralph encouraged others on the team to visit frequently with the programmer—to correlate strategy, to recommend updates, and to consult informally prior to every meeting. Productivity and communication increased.

Metaphors and Pictures

Another helpful reminder is to use the metaphor. How many times have you heard the following:

"There's a monkey on my back."

"It feels like a tight knot in my stomach."

"This problem is beating me up."

"Keep your budget out of the red."

These and many other metaphors are key components of communication for the solution focused manager. Seen as more than just passing phrases, we can use them to enhance communication on a regular basis. Solution focused managers may ask:

"How big is the monkey on your back?"

"Who is tightening the knot?"

"Like the watch in the famous commercial, did we keep on ticking?"

"Did you see it coming?"

"Let's examine some cost-cutting methods."

"Let me help you straighten it out."

"We'll figure out another way together."

Metaphors are used to get something across to us. They help us realize just how good or how bad things are for the other person. Spending time with the exact metaphor communicates our listening and our understanding. But for the solution focused manager, metaphors are more. They hold solutions to problems within them.

What problem does the monkey represent? How big is it? What is it doing? These questions lead to valuable clues about the real issue a person is experiencing.

"This problem is beating me up" gives us a good view of what the person feels, thinks, and how he or she is likely to behave. What to do at this point can come from common sense, discussion, and creating alternatives.

The solution focused manager needs to push for this information, however, because although we often use metaphors we tend not to take them seriously.

California psychologist, Richard Royal Kopp, calls this process "listening with a third eye." (How's that for a metaphor!) He recalls one blustery manager who spoke with passion about having to deal with a project that was "like a wild lion" for him. Kopp coolly replied, "Yes, every lion tamer needs one." The manager lit up and simply said, "Now I know what to do!"

One of our participants at a secretarial seminar was quite concerned with the possibility of making a mistake—a big one—that would jeopardize her boss and her career. "I know I can do this job well, but I worry like crazy that I can't," she confided.

"Don't worry," we counseled, "let's plan the disaster. What would have to happen to completely screw this thing up? What exactly would you have to do to ensure a failure?" Taken aback a bit, she slowly related a step-by-step recipe for failure. When she finished, it was a masterpiece of error, failure, and disaster. We then asked, "How well are you doing each one of those things?" "I'm not," she said in a startled way. After a brief silence, she said, "Thanks. I guess I would be crazy to worry it would happen if I'm not doing what's necessary for it to happen!"

Imagery is remembered. Kopp has stated that the mind remembers images 90-92 percent more than it remembers words. When you want to harvest what's on the inside of your staff and have them (and you) remember it for action, try the metaphor. Kopp recommends:

1. *Notice the metaphor.* "You mentioned this 'tiger by the tail,' Bill."
2. *Explore it.* "Tell me more about how this 'python' is squeezing the breath out of you."
3. *Interpret it.* "Could it be, Bob, that when you say 'we're fishing without bait,' you believe we are ill-prepared, or do you feel we simply forgot the basics?"
4. *Invite a change.* "If you could change things with this 'boulder going uphill,' Helen, what would you change?"
5. *Suggest.* "What if, Cheryl, you had someone help you 'untie the knot' in your stomach? How could that help?"
6. *Relate to the real life situation.* "Now, Bill, if you still hold tight to the 'tiger's tail,' what do you need me to do to help?"

> *Watch your tone of voice.*
> *Make requests reasonable and sparse*
> *. . . and always give a choice.*

CHAPTER TWENTY-ONE

Tactics That Work

" . . . I always agree with my patients."
—Alfred Adler

Michele Weiner-Davis, Steve deShazer, Bill O'Hanlon, John Walter, and Jane Peller are particularly responsible for the next set of suggestions. While they use these techniques in a psychotherapeutic context, we can use them in our board rooms, our offices, and our factories. Try using some over the next week, then notice what seems to be different.

Different or Better?

The next time you begin a meeting or talk with an employee, ask, "Since we met last time, what have you noticed that's different? Or better?" Starting with this question directs the energy of the other person toward solutions. As they discuss what's different or better, note that your role can be to probe ("How'd we do that?"), to encourage ("I like the way you've begun to tackle this one"), and to collaborate ("As we continue to plan, what would be some small indicators that we're on the right track?").

The advantages of this line of questioning are many. First, people rarely ask what's right, yet that's exactly the information needed in order to proceed along a successful path. Second, this question creates thought in the listener. As you experiment, you'll find some of your listeners will look blankly at you, some will repeat the question, and some will giggle nervously. If the listener resists, your natural temptation is to fill the silence—to restate the question or dismiss it. Instead, use what management consultant and conflict specialist, Robert Bramson, has labeled the "friendly, silent expectant stare." Let them know you do want an answer, a specific answer. Stay with it and you will reap a harvest of answers.

"Different or better" also begins a constructive conversation rather than immediately noticing a problem. In a simple way, it can become an expected routine that helps your staff redirect their energies.

I Don't Know

Have you ever been confounded by the answer, "I don't know"? These three short words can effectively release the other person from responsibility, and place it directly on your shoulders. A real conversation stopper, the "I don't know" can be neutralized as follows:

Manager: So, Jim, I was wondering what you think the problem is.

Jim: (Sheepishly) I don't know.

Manager: Well, what would you say if you did know?

Jim: Well, I . . . I . . . oh, I guess I'd think our deadlines are way off.

Delivered without sarcasm, "What would you say if you did know?" actually helps other people over the hurdle of "I don't know" and creates the opportunity to see beyond what they think they can see.

Much of the art of management is simply facilitating change, and helping people to think creatively in order to help themselves. Management can be very much like the martial arts. We use the energy and momentum of others by simply not getting in their way.

As you listen for the "I don't knows" in your day, you'll hear plenty of opportunities to practice. You may even want to use this technique on yourself the next time *you* say, "I don't know!"

Circular Thinking and Questioning

Inviting dialogue between people in different departments can be a real challenge. A sure way to help others engage in dialogue is termed "circular thinking." Our goal here is to elicit what one thinks the other is thinking. As follows:

VP: We have a problem?

Ralph: I think Joe is undermining my team's efforts on the West Coast.

Joe: We're doing nothing of the sort. My team is just very aggressive, that's all. They make money. They succeed where others fail.

Ralph: Our team doesn't fail. We just need more cooperation.

VP: Joe, what do you think Ralph is thinking when he says his team is being undermined?

Joe: I think he thinks we're out to get him.

VP: Is that right, Ralph?

Ralph: Not really. It just seems as if we're competing instead of cooperating. We do all work for the same company.

VP: Joe, what do you think about what Ralph is thinking?

Joe: Let's see. I guess he's not feeling supported, and his team may resent my team's success.

VP: Ralph?

93

Ralph: Sure, we'd like to be doing better. But I worry about our people having conflicts. It's not good in the long run.

Joe: I agree with you. I'm not sure how to settle them down without killing their enthusiasm, though.

Ralph: I don't mind the enthusiasm, but our territory preference listing is really being disregarded.

Joe: But my people seem to do better with those technical types in the Valley than yours do. Sales is our job.

VP: Joe, knowing Ralph as you do, what do you think he'd be willing to do about this?

The VP redirects the discussion when tensions flare or listening stops as people begin the solution process. The purpose of "guessing" what the other thinks is to bring assumptions out into the open in a simple enough way that each person can easily clarify what they think and what they think their partner thinks. Bingo! Circular thinking.

Pre-Change Change

The next time someone makes an appointment with you to discuss a problem, ask how things have begun to resolve themselves since the appointment was made.

Director: How can I help you, Jane?

Jane: I'm really having a problem with my new secretary. Her attitude is poor and her work is even worse. But she's been here forever; she's a real "fixture," as you know.
I inherited her when Bob's position was eliminated last month. It's been a tough four weeks.

Director: I'm glad you came in so soon to discuss it. Other people who have had similar problems with their staff have noticed this: Between the time they made the appointment with me and the time we met, even though the problem wasn't 100% cleared up, they noticed some positive change during that interval. I was wondering if you, too, have noticed some slight positive change in this situation since you made the appointment to talk with me?

Jane: I don't know if it's significant or not, but things seem to be less tense between us since I called you. She's a bit more "up." It's easier for me, too.

Director: What do you think accounts for this difference?

Jane: I don't know. Maybe I thought I had "done something" by calling you; maybe that helped.

Director: When you're aware you are "doing something," how does that make a difference in the way you are with her?

This technique is especially useful when the interval between making the appointment and having the appointment is at least a few days. Try it even if the interval is only hours.

"Between the time you decided to meet with me and now, how has your thinking begun to change?"

"Between the time you decided to meet with me and now, what have you noticed that strikes you as positive?"

"Between the time you decided to meet with me and now, what has happened that leads you to be optimistic that you'll eventually resolve this?"

Common Sense We Sometimes Forget

- If it works, don't fix it—do more of it.

- If what you're doing hasn't worked, do something different; do anything different.

- If you don't know what works, you'll have a lot of room to experiment with something different, anything different.

- When you are "doing the right thing" and it doesn't work, you're probably not doing the right thing for that particular situation or person.

- Let go of that which is not critical. Mistakes happen!

One executive we know keeps these words of wisdom close at hand, in his appointment book, to refresh himself with common sense when he is in a crisis.

A Way to Practice
1. Notice what happens that you would like to continue and record it at the end of every day. Then review it the next morning.
2. Do something different routinely. Do almost anything differently a lot of the time.
3. Look for small change. Never look for big change.
4. Encourage effort—theirs *and* yours.
5. Learn what techniques others use on you that work for you.

Agreement and Education
When Adler said that he always agreed with his patients, he was declaring sound business knowledge. We'll never move anyone from point A to point B without first going ourselves *to* point A.

The late newspaper columnist Sidney Harris once commented that the best teachers go *to* the student and then gently walk *with* them to wisdom.

This is the heart of the management task. We help others move from point A to B and beyond by being best teachers who agree first.

CHAPTER TWENTY-TWO

Cooperation and the Feeling of Equality

"Anyone who is critical of himself is always critical of others. To be human does not mean to be right, does not mean to be perfect. To be human means to be useful, to make a contribution—not for one's self, but for others—to take what there is and to make the best of it."
—Rudolf Dreikurs

Recall our example earlier in the book of the bucksaw being used as an initiation to marriage. The push/pull of this tool is quite like that used by successful managers.

It is not until the managers are able to convey the cooperative feeling that they truly enlist the cooperation of those managed. Likewise, the requirement for using the same bucksaw is equality. Both partners—though not of the same strength, skills, or backgrounds—must cooperate equally in purpose, effort, and worth, for the task to be accomplished.

As Dreikurs has said, both partners must put in their 100 percent. Equality and cooperation are no longer 50/50 propositions.

This may be the trickiest part of the management business. Though we may have different responsibilities, skills, and training, we are equal in value, worth, and purpose with all of our employees. Communicated regularly to your staff, this principle of equality is what makes exceptional work and Solution Focused Management.

Seek to understand your employees and co-workers the way they understand . . . and more.

They are more like you than unlike you.

Show them your respect and that will induce respect from them.

CHAPTER TWENTY-THREE

Your Answer Is Inside the Question

> *"Cheshire-Puss," said Alice, "would you tell me, please, which way I ought to go from here?"*
>
> *"That depends a good deal on where you want to get to," said the Cat.*
>
> *"I don't much care where . . . " said Alice.*
>
> *"Then it doesn't matter which way you go," said the Cat.*
>
> *" . . . So long as I get somewhere," Alice added as an explanation.*
>
> *"Oh, you're sure to do that," said the Cat, "if you only walk long enough."*
>
> —Lewis Carroll,
> *Alice's Adventures in Wonderland*

In sales, in management, and in any person-to-person enterprise, common sense and experience show us that the way we ask questions will greatly influence the kind and quality of answers we will receive. Inviting an interviewee to "tell me a little about yourself" is a much better starting point for conversation than twenty rapid-fire "who-what-when-where-why-and-how" questions. Questions such as, "In what ways do you think the company has benefitted from this contract?" seem to reveal more useful and specific information than, "Was this contract worth it?" And the angry and obvious, "What happened here?" is better replaced with a calmer and more collaborative, "Let's talk about what happened with an eye to the future."

The answers to questions are a kind of *target* we aim for. Overall, open-ended questions are preferable to closed; calm, to angry; general, to specific. Of course, there are times we need a specific closed answer. "What time is the operation?" and "When do we need to have this data?" are two examples of specific, time-limited questions seeking specific, time-limited answers. But in the business of conversation, collaboration, and communication, we're generally much better off engaging the other person first in a cooperative conversation aimed at a not-too-distant target.

When we look at Solution Focused Management, there are times when that "other person" is ourself. These most important inner decisions require just as much a conversational stance as do our outer ones. And how we ask ourselves the questions will in large measure influence what we'll get for an answer . . . even from ourselves.

Just as a goalkeeper in professional soccer never stops anticipating, reacting, and moving, solution focused managers need to be clear about their questioning techniques. Good questions are the single greatest set of tools a manager has.

The following is a list of what we consider to be good Solution Focused Management questions. We use this list as a quick mental review prior to meetings, decisions, and collaborations.

These traditional Solution Focused Management questions are the best beginnings:

- What's it like when it's *not* like that?

- What's *different* about those times?

- What did *you* do that was different?

- How did you *decide* to do that?

- What small steps would need to happen, even over the next few days, to give you an indication that you're *on the right track*?

Later you could add:

- You say, "It's never been easier." How do you account for that?

- You seem to understand that although few things are ever perfect, you can influence the situation in a more positive way. How did you decide to view it in that particular way?

- I'm sure this situation is not unique; we'll come across it again. What are the key elements we'd better remember in being able to solve it?

To encourage another you might say:

- I especially like . . .

- I'm impressed that . . .

- What strikes me the most is . . .

- May I tell you . . .

In evaluating projects and during performance appraisals, especially as they apply to future behavior, it can be useful to use any or all of the following:

- When you are able to make positive progress in this area, how will you know it?

- How will I know it?

- What will be different?

- What difference will that difference make?

- What are some subtle signs that will tell you and me that this change is happening?
- So now what has to happen for you to be able to begin to . . .

When positive change happens:

- Who's responsible for this?
- How were you able to make this happen . . . (so well . . . so fast . . . so often . . .)?
- How can I help you keep the ball rolling in the right direction?
- How will others know that this change has taken place?
- What do you anticipate to be the major obstacles that might come your way within the next few weeks that might possibly get you off track?
- How will you get yourself back on track if that happens?

For groups:

- What's it like for us when things are going better?
- How's that different?
- What difference will that difference make to us as a group?
- How's a small piece of that already happening?
- What would happen if we did more of that more often?
- What needs to happen to move us forward just *one more step* in the right direction?
- What would some *small indicators* be that would show us we're on the right track?

Beware of traditional problem solving questions that may lead to a dead end. These can be killers:

- What's the problem?

- When did it begin?
- How does that affect you?
- Who else is involved?
- Where do you see the problem in other areas?
- Why do you think it continues to be a problem?
- What alternatives have you tried that haven't worked?
- Why do you suppose they haven't worked?
- Why?

When you need to help someone cope better with a failure or an inevitable human weakness, try these:

- How come things aren't a whole lot worse than this?
- What are you doing that's keeping things at this level rather than letting them get even worse?
- What has been most useful about your approach?
- How has that made a difference?
- If things remain this way for a while, what do you think will happen?
- Then what?
- Then what?
- Then what?

As you experiment with your own questions, be aware of their importance. Begin with single straightforward questions that help you articulate the mental shift to solution focused thinking. As you become aware of this shift in your questions, you'll inevitably notice that there will be a natural shift in the answers you receive . . . and in the solutions you discover!

CHAPTER TWENTY-FOUR

Insuring Success: Some (Almost) Fail-Safe Approaches to Working with Another

"The child is 'set-up' to want to know more!"
—Maria Montessori

When I was working on my first graduate degree, my faculty advisor had me write a 10 page proposal about my 150 page thesis requirement. I still remember the day he said, "Kevin, do a good job on the proposal, and your thesis will be 90 percent written." He helped me do a good job. He rejected my proposal 13 times. Then he died! But he was right. In speaking to my new advisor and in writing the thesis, ninety percent of the work had already been done.

So too, with projects big and small. We ensure a successful venture with planning, forethought, and laboring to make it crystal clear to ourselves first.

To drive this point home, my professor said (on about revision number 11), "These 10 pages should be so clear that you could have your local garage mechanics read it, and they should know what it's all about."

This is as true for the beginning of projects as for the middle of them. Each phase, each new step can be carefully planned *as if* it were a new beginning. Because it is!

As the manager, assume leadership for this task above all else.

- Encourage free-wheeling discussion.
- Seek your secretary's opinion.
- Look at the project from different viewpoints.
- Graphically illustrate the plan.
- Ask others to present their part in a creative way.
- Have shortened meetings to work out the problem.
- Meet more frequently but for less time.
- Use a modified task force to dwell on persistent problems.

As the manager, act *as if* this was the most important phase of the project. Don't be afraid to reject ideas until they are very, very clear.

- Invite others into summary meetings . . . especially if they have absolutely *nothing* to do with the project. This might include:

  ► Cafeteria staff
  ► CEO's secretary
  ► Company librarian
  ► Even the CEO!

If you can't make the project understandable to these people, it isn't ready yet.

In putting this much emphasis on preparation, you'll be setting everyone up for success.

CHAPTER TWENTY-FIVE

The Part He Doesn't Let Out Too Much

At a recent party, I met a man who acted rude, harsh, and blustery. In addition to looking as if he was preoccupied, he wasn't a lot of fun to be with. But there was something in his eyes that looked different than all that. Later that evening I was speaking to his wife, who was visibly upset with his demeanor. I said part of what I observed to her, "He seems hurt or something." She stopped, looked surprised, and replied, "That's the part he doesn't let out too often . . . his dad is dying."

Assuming the best about a person is a good strategy even if you know otherwise. You simply can't lose in most face-to-face business meetings when you assume good about the participants.

This does *not* mean you fail to prepare, blindly trust, avoid negotiating, refuse to seek a change of heart, or fail to win cooperation. It simply means you assume what is good about the other.

When you do this, you'll develop an inner confidence in your communication and, in our experience, the other person will let you see what they don't let out too often.

CHAPTER TWENTY-SIX

We Should Talk More about This

Ever feel pushed or pressured into making a decision? It is at these times that we make critical thinking errors in our planning, our judgment, and our actions.

Try using this phrase when you feel the push, then proactively plan the next move.

"We should talk more about this . . . what is it we need to discuss in more detail in order to resolve this matter?"

With this simple method, any group can go about the business of reassuring themselves as they begin the task of problem solving. And reassurance is precisely what you'll have to plan if you are to get ultimate agreement.

At these times, focus less on truth, negotiations, or compromise, and more on "what would it take to make us feel more comfortable?"

CHAPTER TWENTY-SEVEN

Make the Second Call

Did you ever finish a phone call with a "funny feeling"? The kind of feeling that says things are unfinished, that there is a problem, or simply "oh brother!" We usually brush it off, hope it will go away, or just fume. Try making the second call—right away. Confess to the "funny feeling" and ask, "Should we talk a bit more?"

Trust your inner feelings. In almost every case, you'll end this second call on a high. Managers, co-workers, family, and customers will appreciate your straightforwardness, even if there was nothing wrong in the first place.

Even if they still attempt to cover up, they'll admire your courage and your caring. Make the second call!

CHAPTER TWENTY-EIGHT

When in Doubt, Ask "What Did I Forget?"

Steve deShazer, the family counselor from Milwaukee, prides himself on his ironclad belief that people have all the answers to all of their problems inside of them. The counselor's job is simply to cast light on the solutions that already exist within.

Therefore, after successful counseling, deShazer will occasionally get a phone call from a family seeking a second round of counseling. He hears them say:

• We need a ten-thousand mile checkup.

• We're back to square one.

• Things are worse all of a sudden.

• Not sure why, we just know it's not good.

• Feels like the counseling we went through isn't working.

Instead of scheduling a quick appointment, deShazer asks the same question of all of them: "What are you forgetting to do?"

When they tell him what they forgot, he tells them to keep doing that for another two weeks without an appointment. If they still need help, then he'll see them. Needless to say, he sees few.

When you run into a "back to square one" problem, what did *you* forget to do?

CHAPTER TWENTY-NINE

Take a Mental Sabbatical

Long-term employees at McDonald's are required to take an eight-week paid leave for every ten years of service. The time is theirs to do with as they wish, no strings attached. And they get full pay and benefits as well. Based on the belief that even people need retooling once in a while, this company not only encourages time off . . . it requires it!

Not all of us can afford a sabbatical, but we can arrange for one as part of each day. These "mental sabbaticals" can be as simple as closing your office door or conference room for ten to twenty minutes a day and allowing yourself to daydream. Or get up twenty minutes early and walk, jog, or run on a particularly beautiful road. You could even schedule time for that special hobby, foreign language, or time with the kids that seems to elude you.

The important thing is to make the effort to take the break. For years, college professors, authors, and ministers have seen the value of time-outs to rest and prepare.

Your mental sabbatical will pay you back many-fold. Try it. Then, notice what's better about your life and your work.

CHAPTER THIRTY

Declare Bankruptcy . . . Emotionally That Is!

Next time you're in a fight you simply can't win, know enough to fold up your cards and live to try another day.

Though not a particularly enviable strategy, declaring emotional bankruptcy can be a realistic alternative to frustration, anger, loss of control, and defeat.

Emotional bankruptcy is another "inside job." You need notify no one except yourself. This allows you to take stock, recognize, even move to another issue.

Take care not to confuse bankruptcy with defeat. Bankruptcy recognizes defeat is on the way but stops it soon enough to allow your reserves to help you reorganize and restructure. The following helpful phrases can move the conversation along:

- I see your point.

- Let's give it a try and evaluate it at a later date.

- I'll concede. Yours makes sense.

- You might be right.

- What's the worst thing that can happen?

CHAPTER THIRTY-ONE

How Was I Different Today . . . And What Difference Did That Seem to Make?

This daily approach to self-(and others') improvement is best done at the end of each day. This question focuses on two key aspects. First, what was in fact done. Second, what was different or, at the very least, what *seemed* different.

When we have the benefit of constant feedback, we can make constant adjustments. Driving on an expressway will automatically regulate our speed because of the visual feedback we receive from the cars in front of us or to the sides of us. A car on cruise control only knows one speed. On a busy expressway, that would certainly be disastrous! On the long open stretches of an interstate highway, however, cruise control is a lifesaver.

In sports, coaches can perfect the athlete's skill with a single stream of "yes, yes, yes," "you've got it. Now try . . . " The athletes can then self-correct simultaneously with the instruction.

In like manner, asking this daily question helps you make changes, especially when no direct simultaneous feedback is available. As with other self-techniques, just ask the questions; then notice what works.

"How was I different today . . . and what difference did that make?"

CHAPTER THIRTY-TWO

"When I Treat Him in a More Businesslike Fashion, We Get More Done"

During a recent consultation, a vice-president came up with this statement as his understanding of when things were different with himself and his chief financial officer. Used to a team approach, this vice-president's warm and friendly approach actually worked against him in communicating with an extremely technical financial wizard.

No great psychology here, just valuable experience. Review for yourself, how do the important people in your life seem to respond when you treat them your natural way? And how do they respond when you treat them in a way that seems to be more comfortable *for them*?

CHAPTER THIRTY-THREE

Watch for "The Trance"

- The very best conversationalists,
  - The very best sales people,
    - The very best supervisors,
      - And the very best people persons are the ones who ask good questions . . . *one at a time*.

Take note of interview shows on television and the radio. The very best interviewers ask one question at a time. It sounds easy but, in fact, it's a very developed skill.

Many questioners ask two or more questions in one:

- How long will it take . . . and who's going to do it anyway?

- What do you think? What I mean is, what are the good points?

- What do you think is the down side here? How does your department feel and why do you think that's true?

Some even give an answer in advance:

- What's your estimate . . . one year?

- What do you think . . . the blue and the gold looks pretty good doesn't it?

Some sound like a multiple choice exam:

- If we all move on it, what do you think . . . one year, eight months, six months?
- You think we should, or shouldn't?

  One at a time elicits more thought and better answers.

- I'd like to know how you feel about the proposed merger?
- If you were to decide, which way would you be leaning?
- How do you think we ought to handle the vacancy?
- Tell me why you want to resign?
- Are you O.K.?

When you ask one question at a time, especially solution focused questions, you may notice the other person staring at you. They may not even answer you at first or may even look as if they're in a trance-like state. They might be!

Give them the necessary quiet time to think before they answer. Simply look at them as Bramson recommended in Chapter Twenty-One—give them the friendly, silent, expectant stare.

What they say next may amaze you both. Watch for the "trance" and then let it happen!

> *Look for the good, make the bad good, and use humor.*
>   -Don Dinkmeyer

CHAPTER THIRTY-FOUR

Don't Throw That Old Picture Out . . . Reframe It!

Next time you're in a frame shop, ask the owner to recommend two frames for your picture. One that is absolutely a perfect match and one that's absolutely awful! Same picture. But after you put the frame around it, you'll know the difference a frame can make!

So, too, with the frames we put around people.

- He's lazy.

- She's just weird.

- Ralph makes stupid mistakes.

- Jane is the most belligerent person I know.

Think of the frames you use, especially the negative ones.

Typically these negative frames don't allow us much maneuvering room. A lazy person is just lazy. Not much we can do about that. Weird is weird. There is no excuse for "stupid" mistakes, at least the ones someone *else* makes! And belligerent people are not to be reasoned with.

129

But what if we had another frame?

- He's not lazy, I just think he's very discouraged at the lack of progress he sees.

- He's preoccupied, or he seems confused, or just maybe he's not sufficiently skilled.

- Maybe we need to try and do more training.

- She's not weird, she's just a very creative person who needs more time to present this to us.

- Let's talk to her and see if she's okay.

- She's been under a lot of stress lately.

- He doesn't make stupid mistakes for no reason, I'll bet he isn't aware of what he needs to do.

- I think he'll do better with a bit more one-on-one supervision time.

- Let's ask what help *he* thinks he might need.

The purpose of reframing is not to be "nice" or "charitable" or "optimistic."

We reframe for *us*. It allows us to find a way out, a way to help and effectively manage.

CHAPTER THIRTY-FIVE

Flag
the Minefield

How many times have you started a new project full of vigor and hope, only to encounter problem after problem? Soon you can lose track of the goal and be in terrible shape.

Wouldn't it be easier if you could see the possible problems in advance? Well, you can. During the vigor and hope and optimism, volunteer yourself to become the "wet blanket" for the team.

> "I'd like to suggest we look ahead to the possible difficulties that might come our way with this project and mark them now so we can avoid them later."

This technique injects a realistic caution into exciting projects and further specifies detailed ones. Even when the problems you think might happen do actually happen, they certainly won't be surprises.

Anticipated problems can be planned for. Unanticipated problems can take control easily. Wet blankets are a project's best friends.

131

In the same way you would walk a minefield and carefully place a flag next to each live, unexploded mine, you will want to look at your projects and *flag the minefields*!

CHAPTER THIRTY-SIX

Storm the Back Door

Ever been locked in a conflict head-on with an employee or customer? If you have, you know how frustrating it is to attempt solutions that are rejected or beaten down one after the other. It's as if you're knocking on the front door with no answer.

Try going to the *back* door:

- Find a topic of agreement for both of you.

- Use compliments (genuine ones) generously.

- Bring in a third person, not to mediate but to provide a third perspective.

- Agree with your foe.

- Don't disagree, ask more questions.

- Try to do it their way.

- Talk about their children.

- Talk about their hobby.

- Go to lunch.

- Arrange a business trip together.

- Agree with them!

Any idea you have that gets you away from the front and moves you to the back will help break the deadlock and permit a new way to engage.

CHAPTER THIRTY-SEVEN

Can You Tell the Difference?

Ever find yourself stuck with just one opinion despite your best efforts?

- She's just lazy.

- He's intolerable.

- We're in deep trouble.

- Things are as bad as I've ever seen them.

Try forcing yourself to consider a range of alternatives by asking the "difference question":

- Can you tell if she is lazy or if she's just under such enormous stress that she's paralyzed?

  - And what difference would that make?

- Can you tell the difference between whether he's intolerable or whether he's deeply troubled and preoccupied with his own concerns?

  - And, how would that make a difference in the way you managed him?

- Can you tell the difference between whether we're in deep trouble or we're just in the middle of a very long tunnel? If we keep moving in the same direction, will we see light at the end of the tunnel soon?

  - Therefore, what should we be doing now?

- Can you tell the difference between "Things are as bad as I've ever seen them," and "They really could be much worse"?

  - And what does that tell me?

This "difference question" permits you to see at least two, and sometimes many more, possibilities that can expand your thinking rather than limit it.

Normalize the abnormal.

"If I were you, and knowing what you've gone through, I think I would probably react the same way."

"That doesn't sound so weird to me. You must have been under some incredible stress."

"I don't blame you."

"Sounds about right to me."

"You could have reacted even worse . . . how'd you keep your cool as you did?"

"I'm not as worried about what you did. I want to help both of us fix it."

"You might be right."

CHAPTER THIRTY-EIGHT

To Avoid Failure, Predict the Relapse

Performance appraisals are only valuable if they help change behavior. Even the most valuable employee's evaluation is worth little if it doesn't add to motivation, support, and encouragement. But people rarely change because we tell them to. People change because they tell *themselves* to change.

So next time you're concluding an employee performance appraisal, coaching session, or team building seminar, predict the relapse.

> "It's possible that improvement here isn't always going be perfect. It's possible that as you change things might slip, get worse, even slide. This will be normal. It happens to all of us. When those times happen, how will you know it? What will be some of the first indicators that will tell you it's happening? What do you think you can do at that time?"

In this way, the employee has the permission, the time, and the reassurance to forecast predictable relapses.

As an interesting postscript, the relapses talked about in this way almost never happen in the way we thought they would. And when they *do* happen, we are ready for them!

When things go right, find out who was responsible and blame them . . . profusely and positively.

When things are on schedule, find out why!

When people are doing their jobs, comment! . . . and then find out why.

When the company makes money, use some of it and throw an impromptu party!

Get to the bottom of why things work well and who is responsible, and you'll tap the real secret of your organization.

CHAPTER THIRTY-NINE

Notice What You Notice

This technique is the closest thing to psychological magic yet to be discovered.

"Over the next week notice those things that happened which you would like to have continue to happen. Notice those things between you and the other person that you'd like to have continue. Simply notice them. Then at the end of the week, see what's better or different."

With your colleagues, family, business, customers—and even just within yourself—this "notice technique" can help you tap the solutions that already exist within you.

We're not going to give you examples or testimonials here because we really just want you to try it. We want you to notice for yourself.

And it is simply taking note of what you notice that can make life a richer and more rewarding experience . . . noticing all that life has for us, joining with others in cooperation, and having the courage to move on.

When all else fails?

Remember the solutions that are inside . . . inside of you!

Bibliography and Resources

The following are some very useful resources—books and tapes that you will refer to often.

1. Adler, Alfred. *Cooperation Between the Sexes*. Writings about sex, love, and marriage, edited by Heinz Ansbacher. Chicago: Alfred Adler Institute of Chicago, 1985.

2. Allred, G. Hugh. *Teenagers: A Survival Guide for Mom and Dad*. Salt Lake City: Bookcraft, 1986. (One of the best books about adolescents on the market today. A must for parents of teens.)

3. deShazer, Steve. *Keys to Solution in Brief Therapy*. New York: W. W. Norton, 1985. (The original brief solution focused handbook.)

4. ___. *Clues: Investigating Solutions in Brief Therapy*. New York: W. W. Norton, 1988. (The follow-up book

for brief solution focused therapy. A bit more technical but adds depth to the theory and practice.)

5. ___. *Putting Difference to Work*. New York: W. W. Norton, 1991. (deShazer's latest book. An excellent elaboration on his theory.)

6. Dinkmeyer, Dinkmeyer and Sperry. *Adlerian Counseling and Psychotherapy*. Columbus: Merrill Publishing Company, 1987. (An excellent overview of the psychology of Alfred Adler. Adler spent his professional life working with families and developed a psychology and personality theory that could be understood by the lay person. Rudolf Dreikurs was Adler's disciple in America.)

7. Dreikurs, Rudolf and Soltz, Vicki. *Children The Challenge*. New York: E.P. Dutton, 1987. (A work that was twenty years ahead of its time. Still popular today. A "must-read" for parents . . . and an even "better-read" for managers who want to be ahead of *their* time.)

8. Dreikurs, Rudolf. *Social Equality: The Challenge of Today*. Chicago: The Alfred Adler Institute, 1971. (A classic read. Fifteen years ahead of its time.)

9. Kral, Ron. *Strategies that Work: Techniques for Solutions in the Schools*. Milwaukee: Brief Family Therapy Center, 1988. (A short, very straightforward book for teachers and youth workers. A very fine resource and a quick way to get acquainted with this theory.) Available by calling 414-464-7775.

10. O'Hanlon, William H. and Weiner-Davis, Michele. *In Search of Solutions: A New Direction in Psycho-*

therapy. New York: W. W. Norton, 1989. (A terrific book. Easy to read and chock-full of ideas for those doing counseling, coaching, and consultation. Highly recommended.)

11. Popkin, Michael. *Active Parenting.* San Francisco: Harper and Row, 1987. (One of the best books for families with children of all ages.)

12. Sherman and Dinkmeyer. *Systems of Family Therapy: An Adlerian Integration.* New York: Brunner/Mazel Publishers, 1987. (A good description of the many schools of thought currently being used in family counseling.)

13. Walter, John, and Peller, Jane. *Becoming Solution Focused in Brief Therapy.* New York: Brunner/Mazel, 1992. This is a tremendous book that details the method of focusing on solutions. An excellent book to help make the transition from psychology and psychotherapy to our businesses and boardrooms.

Audio Tapes

These audio tapes are available directly from the authors, Kevin O'Connor (708-577-7044) Fax (708-577-8181), or Frank Bucaro (708-697-1587) or Fax (708-697-1505).

1. "Dissatisfied Customers Never Come Back and Other Myths That Limit Your Success" ($60.00) (Six-cassette album devoted to sales and sales management.)

2. "Thirty Management Tips in Thirty Minutes" ($10.00) (A one-cassette album that can be listened to and re-listened to for motivational and educational purposes.

3. "Sixty Parenting Tips in Sixty Minutes" ($10.00) (A one hour cassette that focuses on the best solutions available for parenting difficult situations.)

4. "Living and Working With (Sometimes) Difficult People" ($10.00) Kevin O'Connor. (Kevin's summary of some of the best strategies from Dreikurs and Alessandra in handling difficult situations at home at work.)

5. "Sudden Solutions to Persistent Problems" ($10.00) Kevin O'Connor. (Kevin's best insights from *When All Else Fails*.)

About the Authors

Bucaro and O'Connor is an independent speaking and consulting firm founded in 1980. Offering adult training, motivational and educational speeches, and confidential corporate consultations, this company custom designs each seminar, speech, and program.

Working as client-focused and solution focused, Bucaro and O'Connor learn the company and the audience first, then develop their presentation. They are known for high-interest, high-quality programs. This team assures quality work with a unique money-back guarantee.

Frank C. Bucaro is an adult trainer, professional speaker, and consultant specializing in management, ethics, and employee potential. Frank gives over a 150 presentations yearly to organizations, professional associations, and corporations. Known for his lively style and strong presentation method, Mr. Bucaro leaves audiences with high-impact programs for immediate use.

Kevin E. O'Connor is a professional speaker, consultant, and trainer, who specializes in conflict management, morale, and leadership. With graduate degrees in Education and Counseling Psychology, Kevin's work centers on professional presentations, speeches, seminars and individual corporate consultations. A specialist in adult learning, Mr. O'Connor is known for his group process skills and high-content presentations that assure participant satisfaction, increased expertise, and the courage to begin necessary change.

Together, Bucaro and O'Connor speak, train, and consult from the "inside-out." Their research and curriculum is focused on the detailed specifics of the company, the task, and the person—thus assuring long-term effectiveness and productivity.

Bucaro & O'Connor are available to consult with you or speak to your group. Please phone Frank Bucaro at (708) 697-1587 or Fax (708-697-1505), Kevin O'Connor at (708) 577-7044, or Fax (708) 577-8181.

Index

A

Adler, Alfred 57, 66, 74, 91, 96
Advice 54
Alternative approaches 133-34
Appraisals, performance 103-04, 139
Assumptions, of good 109-10
Attention 79

B

Bramson, Robert 92
Burton, John 65

C

Carroll, Lewis 101
Change
    personal 45-46
    pre-change 94-95
    smaller to bigger 83-84
Circular thinking 93-94
Coaching 42-43, 54
Collaboration 47-49 (*See also* Teamwork)
Common sense 95-96

Competence 3
Confidence, showing 81
Conflict 41-44, 58, 133-34
Conflict resolution
    family 24-25, 45-46
    workplace 28-31, 43-44
Cooperation 30-31, 57-58, 69-70, 97-98
Copeland, Aaron 37
Corollaries 77-82
    A 79
    B 79-80
    C 80-81
    D 81-82

D

Decision making 111
deShazer, Steve 13, 18-19, 91, 115 (*See also* Miracle question)
Difference question 135-36
Difference, making the 121-22
Different or better 6, 53-54, 91-92
Dinkmeyer, Don 127
Direction 60-61

151

DMS ("Do More of the Same")
    53
Doing nothing 73-74
Dreikurs, Rudolf 8, 41, 51, 55,
    58, 65, 75, 77, 97
DS ("Do Something—But Not
    Much of Something") 76
DSD ("Do Something Different")
    53, 71-72
DTO ("Do the Opposite") 75-76

E

Emotional bankruptcy 119
Emotions 65-67
Employees, motivated 19-20
Encouragement 81-82
Equality 97-98
Erickson 19
Exceptions
    behavioral 53
    to problems 2-3

F

Fear, reduction of 73-74
Feelings 65-67 (*See also* Phone
    call)
Focus 18
    interaction 58-60
    intimidation 59-60
    on self 28-29
Follow through 11-12

G

Goals 62, 77-78

H

Harris, Sidney 96
Help, getting 11
Hidden messages 78-79

Human behavior, principles of
    17-18

I

Imagery 87-88
Implementation 51-54
Impulse 61-62
Independence, stimulation of 82
Inexperience 92-93
Initiative 46
Interaction 59-60
    interpersonal 17
    understanding 123
Interviewing 125-26

J

Junk 45-46

K

Keller, Helen 9
Kopp, Richard Royal 87

L

Labeling 19
Leadership 108
Lewis, C.S. 57

M

Management
    active 58
    new approach to 1-3
Managers 13-15
Meetings
    malaise in 5-6
    productive 14-15
Messages, hidden 78-79
Metaphors 83, 86-88
Miracle question 6, 37-39
Miracles 37-38, 53

Missing elements 115-16
Montessori, Maria 107
More of the Same 24-27

N

Natural strengths 54
Nightingale, Earl 69
Notice technique 143-44

O

O'Hanlon, Bill 91

P

Peacemaker 80-81
Peller, Jane 91
Performance appraisals 103-104, 139
Personality problems 27
Phone access 28-29
Phone call, making a second 113
Popkin, Michael 77, 81
Positive thinking 20
Power 79-80
Practice 96
Problem-free 53
Problems 9-12, 18
    alternatives to 11
    anticipated 131-32
    defined 10-11
    identifying 33-34
    marital 27-28
    personality 27
    resolution of 10-12, 34

Q

Questioning 93-94
Questions, Solution Focused 26-27, 102-05

R

Reassurance, planning 111
Reframing 129-30
Relapses, predictable 139-40
Reminders, helpful 83-84
Review 52
Robinson, Dr. Lee 1

S

Sabbatical, mental 117
Soltz, Vicki 8, 55
Solution Focused Management 1-2, 6-7, 13-14, 17-20, 23-25, 49, 54, 59-60, 98, 102, 158
    applications of 7
    basis of 17
    characteristics of 6-7
    defined 1-2, 13
    lessons of 25-26
    patterns in 23
Solution Focused questions 26-27, 102-05
Solutions 18
    access to 1-2
    blameless 5-6
    defined 6
    existing 2, 85-86
    internal 5-7, 20
    strategies 5-6, 78
Strengths, building on 81
Success 107-08

T

Tactics 91-96
Talents 17
Teamwork 34
Thinking, expanded 136
Time off 117
Training 62-63

U

Unpredictability 53

V

Value, personal 81-82
Visualization 38-39

W

Walter, John 91
Walton, Frank 44
Weiner-Davis, Michele 91
Work partners, uncooperative
    28-31
Wright, Frank Lloyd 23, 34